LANGUAGE EXERCISES

FOR ADULTS

Betty Jones
Saranna Moeller
Cynthia T. Strauch

Consultants

John Ritter
Master Teacher
Oregon Women's Correctional Center
Salem, Oregon

Dannette S. Queen
Adult Education
New York City Board of Education
Bronx, New York

STECK-VAUGHN
C O M P A N Y
ELEMENTARY · SECONDARY · ADULT · LIBRARY

Acknowledgments

Executive Editor: Diane Sharpe
Supervising Editor: Stephanie Muller
Project Editor: Patricia Claney
Design Manager: Richard Balsam

Photography: Leslie Bowen, Cooke Photographic, Bob Daemmrich, Mike Flahive, Phyllis Liedeker, Beverly Logan, Kurt Johnson, James Minor, David Omer, Michael Patrick, Rick Patrick, Bill Records, Park Street, R David Taylor, and Sandy Wilson.

Stock Photography:

P.1 (jet) Courtesy Grumman History Center; (helicopter) Courtesy Bell Helicopter; (car) Courtesy Ford Motor Corporation; p.8 (cat) © Michael & Barbara Reed/Animals Animals; (kitten) © Breck P. Kent/Animals Animals; p.9 (antelope) Courtesy US Wildlife Service; (seal) © Patti Murray/Animals Animals; (car) Courtesy Ford Motor Corporation; (jeep) © PhotoEdit; (bread) © Scott Huber; p.10 (man) © PhotoEdit; (woman) © Unicorn; (nurse) © Arnie Katz/Unicorn; (goat) © Cindi Ellis; (otter) © Fred Whitehead/Animals Animals; p.12 (car) Courtesy Ford Motor Corporation; (bus) © Richard Balsam; p.13 (man with fencing) © Anestis Diakopoulos/Stock Boston; (firefighter) © David Carmack/Stock Boston; (welding) Courtesy Portec Inc.; (train) Courtesy Florida State News Bureau; (rose) Courtesy Texas Highways; (dog) © Cindi Ellis; p.15 (grasshopper) © Cindi Ellis; p.21 (elephant) © Zoological Society of San Diego; (nurse) © Arnie Katz/Unicorn; p.22 (dogwood) Courtesy Texas Highways; p.24 (jet) Courtesy Gruman History Center; p.25 (fireworks) Texas Highways; (quarterback) © Tony Freeman/PhotoEdit; (cheerleader) © John O Hagan/Photo Researchers; (telephone) Courtesy AT&T; p.27 © Frank Cezus/FPG; p.32 (bat) © Oxford Scientific Films/Animals Animals; (mechanics) © Barbara Filet/Tony Stone Worldwide; p.35 (fly) © D R Specker/Animals Animals; (pitcher) © John Swait/Allsport; (plane) Courtesy The National Archives; p.36 (student) © Uniphoto; p.49 (horse) © Cindi Ellis; (cat & squirrel) © Superstock; p.51 Courtesy New York Visitor's Bureau; p.54 (nest) © Patti Murray/Animals Animals; p.68 (crowd) © Joan Menschenfreund; p.69 (girl with dog) Joel Schwartz; p.76 (iguana) © Cindi Ellis; (cat) © Michael & Barbara Reed/Animals Animals; p.95 (ship) © Dennis MacDonald/Unicorn; p.95 (ship) © Dennis MacDonald/Unicorn; p.100 (football) Wilson Sporting Goods Company; (basketball) Wilson Sporting Goods Company; p.103 (bat) © Oxford Scientific Films/Animals Animals; (dog) © Cindi Ellis.

LANGUAGE EXERCISES Series:

Level A	Level D	Level G
Level B	Level E	Level H
Level C	Level F	Review

ISBN 0-8114-7875-0

Table of Contents

Unit 5 — Capitalization and Punctuation

Unit 6 — Composition

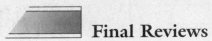

Final Reviews

A. Follow the directions given in each box.

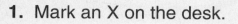

1. Mark an <u>X</u> on the desk. 	**3.** Mark an <u>X</u> over the desk. 
2. Mark an <u>X</u> to the right of the desk. 	**4.** Draw a circle around the desk. 

B. Circle the three things that are alike in some way.

C. Circle the photo that has a missing part. Draw the missing part.

Check What You Know.   Read the directions with the students.

D. Circle the photo that is facing a different way.

E. Read the story. Then number the photos in the correct order.

Lena went to the store. First, she picked up some milk. Then she chose some vegetables. Finally, she got some bread.

_____   _____   _____

F. Write the missing letters.

1. B ____ D ____ F G ____ ____ J ____

2. ____ R ____ T ____ ____ W X ____ ____

3. r ____ t ____ ____ w x ____ ____

4. ____ d ____ f g ____ ____ j k ____

G. Write the words in alphabetical order.

1. Jake _____   2. toe _____

   Darrell _____   eye _____

   Adam _____   nose _____

Check What You Know.   Read the directions with the students.

2

H. Read the words in the box. Then follow the directions.

thin	fan	happy	up	shoe	little

1. Write the word from the box that rhymes with each word.

   new _____   can _____

2. Write the word from the box that means almost the same as each word.

   small _____   glad _____

3. Write the word from the box that means the opposite of each word.

   down _____   thick _____

I. Write to or two to complete each sentence.

1. I like _____ listen to music.

2. I have _____ new tapes.

J. Write T before the telling sentence. Write A before the asking sentence. Write X before the group of words that is not a sentence. Circle the naming words, and underline the action words in each sentence.

_____ 1. Can you go to the store for me?

_____ 2. I need eggs and bread.

_____ 3. to get more soap

K. Circle the special naming words. Underline the action words. Write T before the sentence that has an action word for today. Write Y before the sentence that has an action word for yesterday.

_____ 1. Mr. Kelso helps at Bayview Hospital.

_____ 2. He lives close to the hospital.

_____ 3. Last year Mrs. Kelso worked at the hospital.

_____ 4. She retired this year.

Check What You Know.   Read the directions with the students.

3

L. Circle the word that best completes each sentence.

1. Paul and I (was, were) not home last night.

2. (We, They) had to work.

3. Paul and I have (a, an) evening off next week.

4. Paul and I (is, are) going out to dinner.

M. Circle each letter that should be a capital letter. Add the correct punctuation mark at the end of each sentence.

1. kendall and i shopped at sunshine mall last thursday

2. rosa has not been there since december

3. is that where rosa got her dog, brownie

N. Write complete sentences to answer the questions.

1. Do you like walking or driving?

   _____

2. Do you like to shop at the book store or the music store?

   _____

Below is a list of the sections on *Check What You Know* and the pages on which the skills in each section are taught. If you missed any questions, turn to the pages listed, and practice the skills. Then correct the problems you missed on *Check What You Know.*

Check What You Know. Read the directions with the students. Help students use the *Check What You Know Correlation Chart* to assess the skills they need to work on.

■ **Follow the directions given in each box.**

1. Mark an X on the pot.

5. Mark an X to the left of the pot.

2. Mark an X above the pot.

6. Mark an X inside the pot.

3. Mark an X below the pot.

7. Mark an X on the handle of the pot.

4. Mark an X to the right of the pot.

8. Draw a circle around the pot.

Unit 1, Study Skills. Read the directions with the students. Have students mark an *X* in the following
locations: Box 1: on the pot; Box 2: above it; Box 3: below it; Box 4: to the right of it; Box 5: to the left of it;
Box 6: inside it; Box 7: on the handle. Have students draw a circle around the pot in Box 8.

5

left

right

- **Draw a circle around the correct photo.**

1. Circle the book on the left.

2. Circle the watch on the right.

3. Circle the rose on the left.

4. Circle the clock on the left.

5. Circle the toaster on the right.

Unit 1, Study Skills. Read the directions with the students. Tell students to follow the directions as you tell them which photo to circle in each row. Row 1: the book on the left; Row 2: the watch on the right; Row 3: the rose on the left; Row 4: the clock on the left; Row 5: the toaster on the right.

■ **Look at the photos in each row. Circle the one that is the same as the first photo.**

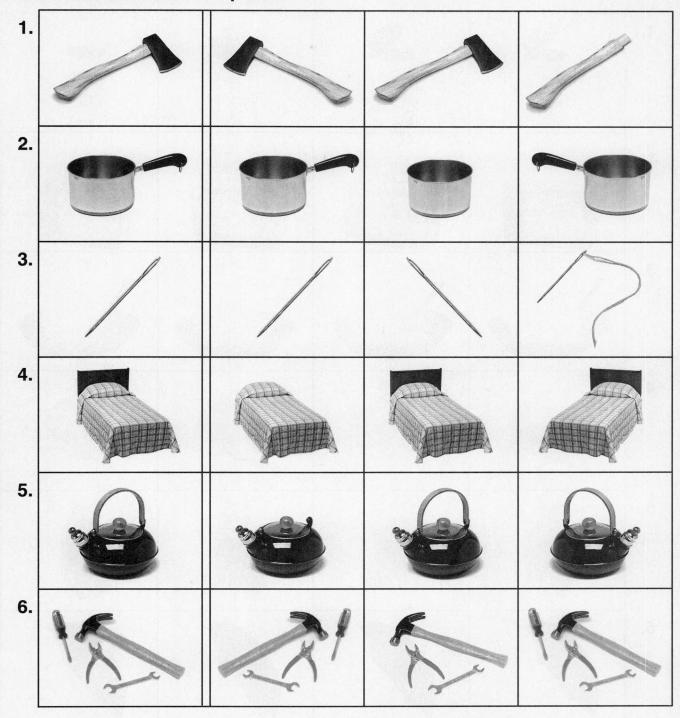

Unit 1, Study Skills. Read the directions with the students. Have students look at the first photo in each row. Tell students to circle another photo in the row that is exactly the same as the first photo.

7

■ **Look at the photos in each row. Circle the one that is different.**

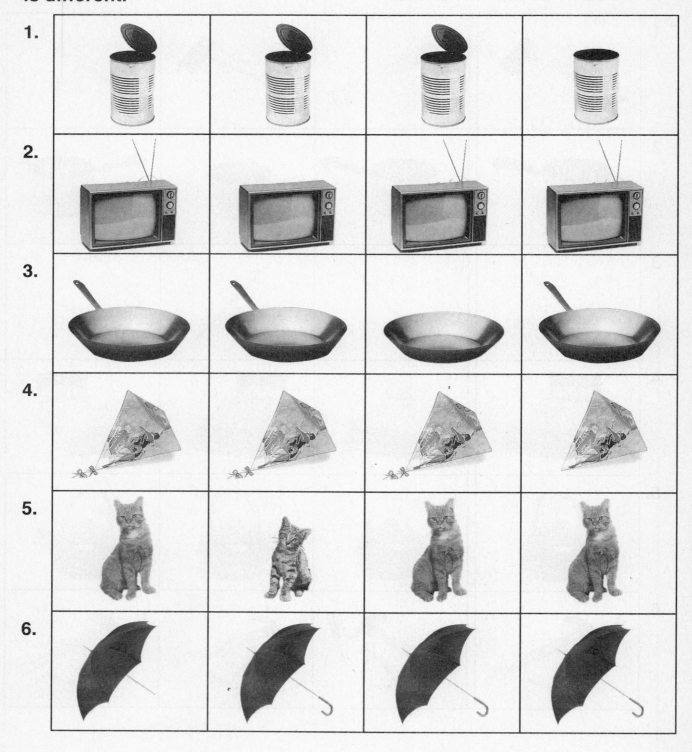

Unit 1, Study Skills. Read the directions with the students. Have students look at the photos in each row, decide which one is different, and circle the different one.

- **Look at the photos. In each row, circle the object in the small box that goes with the group in the large box.**

1.

2.

3.

4.

5.

Unit 1, Study Skills.   Read the directions with the students. Have students name the objects in each row.
Ask how the three objects in the large box are alike. Have students circle the object in the small box that
goes with the group in the large box.

- **Look at the photos in each row. Circle the three things that are alike in some way.**

1.

2.

3.

4.

5.

10

Unit 1, Study Skills.   Read the directions with the students. Have students name the objects in each row. Then have them circle the three objects in each row that are alike in some way.

■ **Look at the photos in each row. Circle the one that has a missing part. Then draw the missing part.**

1.

2.

3.

4.

5.

Unit 1, Study Skills.   Read the directions with the students. Have students examine the photos in each row. Have them circle the one that is missing a part. Then have them draw the missing part.

11

■ **Look at the objects in each row. Circle the one that is facing a different way.**

1.

2.

3.

4.

5.

Unit 1, Study Skills. Read the directions with the students. In each row have students find the object that is facing a different way. Have them circle that photo.

■ **With a partner, read the sentences. Then put an X on the photo that best answers each question.**

1. Bob is sleeping. It is time to wake up. Where is Bob?

2. Frank is ready for work. He goes to the bus stop. He gets on the bus. How does Frank get to work?

3. Jim is a welder. He works with metal. He uses a flame to cut the metal. Where does Jim work?

4. Dan is going home. He stops at a store. He buys some food. Where does Dan go after work?

Unit 1, Study Skills. Read the directions with the students. Have students read each item and the question that follows with a partner. Have students circle the photo that answers each question.

13

■ **Read each story. Then number the photos in the correct order.**

---

1. Robert works on his car. It will not run. Next, he walks to school with his books. Then he studies at the library. Finally, he goes to work. He makes pizza.

____

____

____

____

---

2. Julia rents a house. There is a leak in the roof. First, she calls the man who owns the house. Then he comes to see the leak. Next, a man with a ladder comes to fix the leak. Finally, a friend comes to see Julia.

____

____

____

____

Unit 1, Study Skills. Read the directions with the students. Have them read each story and number the photos to show the order of events.

■ **With a partner, read each sentence. Then mark an X
   on the photo that best answers each question.**

1. Tony made breakfast.
What did he put juice in?

5. Sam spilled water on the floor.
What did he use to clean it up?

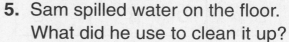

2. Alice wanted shade in her yard.
What did she plant?

6. Mr. Chan sliced an apple.
What did he use?

3. Ms. Flynn picked some flowers.
What did she put them in?

7. Omar wanted to write a note.
With what did he write?

4. Amy made a sandwich.
What did she use?

8. Ramón brought dinner home.
What did he bring?

Unit 1, Study Skills.   Read the directions with the students. Have partners read each sentence and mark
an *X* on the photo that answers each question.

Comparing Letters

- **Circle the capital letter in the large box that is like the one in the small box.**

1. B | D   B   P   S
2. I | T   I   L   N
3. O | O   Q   C   Z
4. E | F   E   H   J
5. C | C   G   O   A
6. N | M   N   W   Q

7. P | R   B   H   P
8. U | U   V   W   K
9. T | F   A   E   T
10. Q | O   Q   C   D
11. W | M   V   W   N
12. D | D   P   C   B

- **Circle the small letter in the large box that is like the one in the small box.**

1. b | k   d   b   p
2. t | g   t   h   r
3. v | w   u   v   z
4. r | m   r   n   f
5. g | y   g   a   j
6. m | s   w   n   m

7. f | h   t   f   k
8. q | p   d   q   b
9. n | m   u   n   h
10. e | e   c   v   z
11. y | q   v   y   g
12. h | f   h   k   d

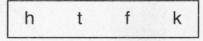

Unit 1, Study Skills.   Read the directions with the students. In the top exercise, have students name the capital letter in the small box and circle the letter in the large box that is exactly like the first. Follow the same procedure with the small letters at the bottom of the page.

A B C D E F G H I J K L M N O P Q R S T U V W X Y Z

■ **Write the missing capital letters.**

A ___ C ___ E ___   ___ B ___ D ___

G ___ I ___ K ___   F ___ H ___ J ___

M ___ O ___ Q ___   L ___ N ___ P ___

S ___ U ___ W ___   R ___ T ___ V ___

Y ___   X ___ Z

A B ___ ___ E F ___   A ___ ___ ___ E ___ ___

___ I ___ ___ L ___   ___ I ___ ___ ___ M ___

O ___ ___ R S ___ ___   ___ ___ ___ Q ___ ___ ___ U

___ ___ X ___ Z   ___ ___ ___ Y Z

a b c d e f g h i j k l m n o p q r s t u v w x y z

■ **Write the missing small letters.**

a ____ c ____ e ____   ____ b ____ d ____

g ____ i ____ k ____   f ____ h ____ j ____

m ____ o ____ q ____   l ____ n ____ p ____

s ____ u ____ w ____   r ____ t ____ v ____

y ____   x ____ z

a ____ ____ d e ____ g   a ____ ____ ____ e ____ ____

____ i ____ ____ ____ n   ____ i ____ ____ ____ m ____

o ____ ____ r ____ t   ____ ____ ____ q ____ ____ ____ u

____ v ____ ____ ____ z   ____ ____ ____ ____ y z

Unit 1, Study Skills.   Read the directions with the students. Have students pronounce the letter names in order. Then have them write the missing small letters on the lines.

A B C D E F G H I J K L M N O P Q R S T U V W X Y Z

■ **Write the missing capital letters.**

1. A _____   3. G _____   5. _____ R   7. _____ M   9. Q _____

2. X _____   4. _____ D   6. _____ K   8. Y _____   10. P _____

11. B _____ D _____   14. G H _____ _____   17. V W _____ _____

12. M N _____ _____   15. J _____ L _____   18. T U _____ _____

13. S _____ _____ V   16. P _____ _____ S

a b c d e f g h i j k l m n o p q r s t u v w x y z

■ **Write the missing small letters.**

1. b _____   3. t _____   5. _____ k   7. _____ u   9. n _____

2. g _____   4. _____ q   6. _____ c   8. e _____   10. y _____

11. c d _____ _____   14. f g _____ _____   17. t _____ _____ w

12. p _____ r   15. h _____ j _____   18. o _____ q _____

13. m _____ _____ p   16. e f _____ _____

Unit 1, Study Skills.   Read the directions with the students. Have students read the letters across the top of the page. Then have them write the missing letters in the answer blanks.

■ **Write the words in alphabetical order.**

1. a b c d e f

cat _____

bird _____

dog _____

frog _____

4. e f g h i j

give _____

help _____

find _____

is _____

2. i j k l m n

know _____

me _____

like _____

just _____

5. l m n o p q

on _____

left _____

near _____

quick _____

3. q r s t u v w x y z

we _____

she _____

they _____

you _____

6. m n o p q r s

red _____

one _____

name _____

most _____

Unit 1, Study Skills.   Read the directions with the students. Have students look at the first four words and the underlined letters. Ask students which of these letters comes first in the alphabet. Have students determine the alphabetical order of the words. Repeat for the other groups.

- **Circle the things that are alike in some way.**

1.

- **Circle the one that does not belong in the group.**

2.

- **Mark an X on the one that is different.**

3.

- **Circle the one that is missing a part. Then draw the missing part.**

4.

- **Mark an X on the one that is facing a different way.**

5.

6.

Unit 1, Study Skills. Review the skills taught in Lessons 1–8 with the students. Then read the directions with the students.

21

- **Read the story. Then number the photos in the correct order.**

  1. Dr. Jansen is busy today. First, she sees Carlos. He does not feel well. Then Mei comes to see the doctor. She has hurt her ankle. Finally, Dr. Jansen asks Sarah if she's feeling better.

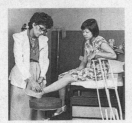 _____  _____ 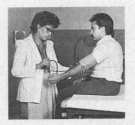 _____

- **Circle the letters that are the same.**

  2. M N M W

- **Circle the letter to the left of the C.**

  3. B C D E

- **Mark an X on the letter that is different.**

  4. q p q q

- **Circle the letter to the right of the h.**

  5. g h i j

- **Write the missing letters.**

  1. C D _____   **3.** Q _____ S   **5.** m n _____

  2. G H _____   **4.** a _____ c   **6.** v _____ x

- **Write the words in alphabetical order.**

  1. in _____   **2.** go _____

  on _____   turn _____

  at _____   stop _____

Unit 1, Study Skills. Read the directions with the students. Have them read the story at the top of the page and number the photos in the correct order. Then have them follow the directions for 2–5. Have them write the missing letters. Finally, have them write the words at the bottom of the page in alphabetical order.

22

▪ **Look at each photo. Then follow the directions.**

1. Mark an X on top of the computer.

2. Mark an X on the chair that is different.

3. Circle the notebooks that are the same.

1. Mark an X on the envelope that is different.

2. Mark an X on the eraser that is facing a different way.

3. Draw a box around the disks that are the same.

Unit 1, Study Skills. Have students look at and name the objects in each photo. Then read the directions with the students.

- **Read each sentence. Then mark an <u>X</u> on the photo that answers each question.**

1. It was a cool day.
   What did Mike put on?

2. Tina works downtown.
   How does she get there?

- **Write the missing capital letters.**

1. A _____   **4.** E _____   **7.** F _____ H

2. M _____   **5.** N _____   **8.** V _____ X

3. Q _____   **6.** R _____   **9.** D _____ F

- **Write the missing small letters.**

1. g _____   **4.** b _____   **7.** m _____ o

2. p _____   **5.** l _____   **8.** s _____ u

3. y _____   **6.** h _____   **9.** a _____ c

- **Write the names in alphabetical order.**

1. Pat _____   **2.** Lynn _____

   Anna _____   Raul _____

   Tom _____   Ellen _____

Unit 1, Study Skills.   Have students tell what is in each of the photos at the top of the page. Then read the directions with the students.

Lesson 17

Naming Sounds

- **Circle the photo that answers each question.**

1. Which do you hear when you unlock the door?

2. Which do you hear when you boil water?

3. Which do you hear when a friend calls?

4. Which do you hear when you play music?

5. Which do you hear at a football game?

6. Which do you hear when someone has a cold?

7. Which do you hear when you are going to the tenth floor?

8. Which do you hear when someone needs help?

Unit 2, Vocabulary. Read the directions with the students. Have students name the photos in each box. Then have students circle the photo that answers each question.

25

■ **Draw a line to connect each pair of objects that rhyme.**

1.

2.

3.

4.

5.

6.

Unit 2, Vocabulary.   Read the directions with the students. Have students say the name of each object in the photos. Have them draw a line from the object in the first column to the object shown in the second column that ends with the same sound.

■ **Write the word that rhymes with the word in bold.**

1. Ted went to the **shop**

To buy a new _____ . (map, mop)

2. A tall young **man**

Turned on the _____ . (fan, fin)

3. Our old gray **cat**

Lay on a soft _____ . (mop, mat)

4. The black-and-white **bug**

Went under the _____ . (rug, rag)

5. A big green **frog**

Sat on a _____ . (log, lap)

6. It is lots of **fun**

To walk in the _____ . (sand, sun)

7. I went with my **date**

Through the open _____ . (goat, gate)

Unit 2, Vocabulary.   Read the directions with the students. Then read each rhyme and the two word choices together. Then have students decide which word at the right rhymes with the word in dark print. Have students write the rhyming word on the lines.

27

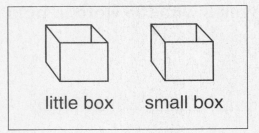

little box   small box

■ **Circle the two words that mean almost the same.**

1. little   big   small   7. look   see   book

2. one   start   begin   8. large   big   little

3. stop   start   finish   9. up   below   under

4. sound   give   noise   10. all   every   one

5. high   down   tall   11. happy   sad   glad

6. wide   narrow   thin   12. easy   hard   simple

■ **Read the sentences. Circle the word that means almost the same as the underlined word.**

1. My book is on the little table.   (small, big)

2. It is a large book.   (red, big)

3. It is about fixing cars.   (breaking, repairing)

4. My papers are under the book.   (on, below)

5. You can print in my book.   (see, write)

6. Now you can stop looking at it.   (finish, be)

7. I will start reading my book.   (be, begin)

8. I won't make a sound.   (noise, picture)

Unit 2, Vocabulary.   Read the directions with the students. Tell them that the words in the box mean almost the same. Have them circle the two words that mean almost the same at the top of the page. Then have them circle the word that means almost the same as the underlined word at the bottom of the page.

Writing Words with Like Meanings

■ **Read each pair of sentences. Circle the word in the second sentence that means almost the same as the underlined word. Then write the words that mean almost the same.**

1. I hear a <u>sound</u>. The noise is my TV.

   _____   _____

2. I <u>begin</u> to turn it off. My wife starts to enjoy the show.

   _____   _____

3. She wants to <u>see</u> this show. I will watch it with her.

   _____   _____

4. She is <u>glad</u> that I will join her. I am happy to be with her, too.

   _____   _____

5. The show has <u>ended</u>. We are finished watching TV.

   _____   _____

6. Tiger is a <u>little</u> cat. He is small for his age.

   _____   _____

7. He <u>likes</u> to play outside. He enjoys looking at things.

   _____   _____

8. Tiger <u>heard</u> a sound. He listened to the noise.

   _____   _____

9. The cat ran <u>under</u> a tree. He was below a nest.

   _____   _____

10. A <u>big</u> bird looked down. The large bird chased Tiger.

    _____   _____

Unit 2, Vocabulary.   Read the directions with the students. Have students circle a word in the second sentence that means almost the same as the underlined word in the first sentence. Have them write the two words on the lines.

29

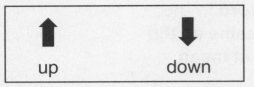

- **Draw lines to connect the pairs of words that are opposites.**

1.	on	dark	**3.**	sink	thick
	hard	down		tall	back
	up	soft		thin	float
	light	off		front	short

2.	in	out	**4.**	good	dry
	many	old		wide	bad
	go	one		find	lose
	new	come		wet	narrow

- **Read the sentences. Circle the word that is the opposite of the underlined word.**

   1. Peter came in the front door.   (inside, back)
   2. He put on some old clothes.   (dry, new)
   3. He made the house look clean.   (wide, dirty)
   4. Peter felt happy.   (sad, late)
   5. Then he went up the stairs.   (down, out)
   6. He sat on his soft bed.   (new, hard)
   7. It was dark outside.   (light, cold)
   8. He turned on the lamp.   (red, off)

Unit 2, Vocabulary.   Read the directions with the students. Tell them that the words at the top of the page are opposites. Have students choose the words that are opposites and connect them. Then have them read the sentences and circle the word that is the opposite of the underlined word.

tall	down	later	in	light
new	night	out	soft	closed

- **Find the word from the box that means the opposite of the underlined word. Write the opposites on the lines.**

1. I am <u>short</u>, and my friend is ___ .

   _____ _____

2. She has <u>dark</u> hair, and I have ___ hair.

   _____ _____

3. When I <u>opened</u> the door, she ___ it.

   _____ _____

4. When I go <u>out</u>, she comes ___ .

   _____ _____

5. Her car is <u>old</u>, but mine is ___ .

   _____ _____

6. First, I get <u>in</u> my car, and then I get ___ .

   _____ _____

7. At work, I go <u>up</u> the steps and ___ the ramp.

   _____ _____

8. I have a <u>hard</u> apple and a ___ cookie with my lunch.

   _____ _____

9. I will eat one <u>now</u> and save the other for ___ .

   _____ _____

10. I work all <u>day</u> and sleep all ___ .

    _____ _____

Unit 2, Vocabulary.   Read the directions with the students. Have students choose an opposite for each underlined word. Then write the two opposites on the lines.

31

bat   a.   b.   duck   a.   b.

■ **Write the letter of the correct meaning.**

_____ **1.** The woman hit the ball with a <u>bat</u>.

_____ **2.** The <u>bat</u> likes the dark.

_____ **3.** Mr. Mata plays ball with a heavy <u>bat</u>.

_____ **4.** He wants to know how a <u>bat</u> sees at night.

_____ **5.** I'll buy a new glove and <u>bat</u>.

_____ **6.** A <u>bat</u> is a mammal.

_____ **7.** I read a book about <u>bats</u> that live in New Mexico.

_____ **8.** I saw that <u>duck</u> catch a fish.

_____ **9.** There was a <u>duck</u> with four ducklings on the pond.

_____ **10.** We had to <u>duck</u> under a fence.

_____ **11.** We were asked to <u>duck</u> so the people behind us could see.

_____ **12.** The <u>duck</u> swam in the water.

_____ **13.** The tall man had to <u>duck</u> to get through the door.

_____ **14.** The boxer had to <u>duck</u> quickly.

Unit 2, Vocabulary. Read the directions with the students. Have students look at the words at the top of the page and the pairs of photos that show the different meanings of the words. Then read each sentence together, and have students write the letter of the correct meaning in each space.

Lesson 25

Writing Words That Sound Alike

- **Write each sentence using to.**

  1. I took a chair ___ Ben.

  2. Ben came over ___ eat dinner.

  3. He will wait ___ eat dessert.

  4. He wants ___ help wash the dishes.

- **Write each sentence using two.**

  1. There are ___ women.

  2. They have worked together for ___ years.

  3. They each have ___ meetings.

  4. They need to have ___ things ready for the meetings.

- **Circle to or two to complete each sentence.**

  1. I have (two, to) sets of tools.

  2. I use them (two, to) do my job.

  3. I work in (two, to) different buildings.

  4. I walk from one building (two, to) the other each day.

Unit 2, Vocabulary. Read the directions with the students. Review the meanings of *to* and *two*. Have students add *to* or *two* to each incomplete sentence, and then write the complete sentence. Then have students circle the correct word in each sentence at the bottom of the page.

33

▪ **Mark an X on the photo that answers each question.**

1. Which do you hear when you are getting dressed?	2. Which do you hear when your boss calls?

▪ **Circle the words that rhyme.**

1.	star	car	bat		5.	door	mouse	house
2.	log	hat	fog		6.	sat	hat	sit
3.	tug	rug	big		7.	ran	run	sun
4.	boat	float	cap		8.	when	pants	ten

▪ **Draw lines to connect the words that are opposites.**

1.	hard	down		2.	in	dark
	up	new			go	out
	old	soft			light	come
	push	pull			on	off

▪ **Draw lines to connect the words that mean almost the same.**

1.	little	big		2.	sound	see
	stop	end			look	noise
	large	small			print	under
	start	begin			below	write

---

34   **Unit 2, Vocabulary.**   Review the activities for sounds in Lesson 17, for rhyming words in Lessons 18 and 19, for opposites in Lessons 22 and 23, and for words that mean the same in Lessons 20 and 21. Then read the directions with the students.

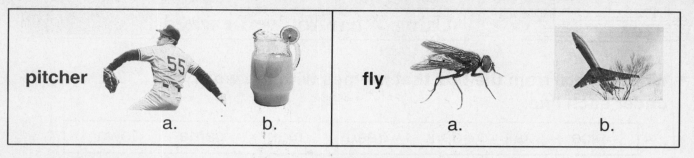

pitcher			fly		
	a.	b.		a.	b.

- **Write the letter of the correct meaning.**

_____ **1.** I will put water in the <u>pitcher</u>.

_____ **2.** The <u>pitcher</u> threw three strikes in a row.

_____ **3.** The <u>pitcher</u> of juice is almost empty.

_____ **4.** That man is a good <u>pitcher</u>.

_____ **5.** I like to <u>fly</u> in a plane.

_____ **6.** A <u>fly</u> came in the open door.

_____ **7.** A <u>fly</u> is an insect.

_____ **8.** Did you see the geese <u>fly</u> south?

- **Complete each sentence using <u>to</u> or <u>two</u>.**

1. Ms. Rosen has _____ books.   (two, to)

2. She went _____ school.   (two, to)

3. She likes _____ read.   (two, to)

4. Her _____ children also like to read.   (two, to)

5. Ms. Rosen took her children _____ the library.   (two, to)

6. They each checked out _____ books.   (two, to)

7. Then they went back _____ their house.   (two, to)

8. It was almost time _____ eat dinner.   (two, to)

Unit 2, Vocabulary.   Review Lessons 24 and 25. Then read the directions with the students.

■ **Write a word from the box that rhymes with the word under each line.**

| nice | tall | dark | read | man | came | town |

1. Mr. Kent is the new _____ in class.
   fan

2. He _____ last week.
   same

3. He moved into _____ last month.
   crown

4. He is a _____ man with long legs.
   call

5. He has _____ hair.
   mark

6. He seems very friendly and _____.
   rice

7. Mr. Kent likes to _____ books.
   seed

■ **Complete each sentence using two or to.**

1. I met _____ friends at the show.

2. We wanted _____ see a good movie.

3. We bought _____ hot dogs and a soda.

4. We tried _____ find the best seats.

5. We had _____ minutes to find our seats.

6. The movie started at _____ o'clock.

7. My friends had _____ go home after the movie.

Unit 2, Vocabulary. Read the directions with the students. Then read the sentences at the top of the page together, and have students write the word from the box that rhymes with the word below the lines. Then have students write *two* or *to* for the sentences at the bottom of the page.

say	large	go	thin	see	day	stop	log
me	bumpy	small	glad	new	off	look	bug
man	soft	high	out	big	close	mat	down

- **Write the words from the box that rhyme.**

  1. book _____

  2. say _____

  3. dog _____

  4. dig _____

  5. fan _____

  6. rug _____

  7. see _____

  8. cat _____

- **Write the words from the box that mean almost the same.**

  1. look _____

  2. little _____

  3. tall _____

  4. happy _____

  5. skinny _____

  6. tell _____

  7. near _____

  8. big _____

- **Write the words from the box that mean the opposite.**

  1. on _____

  2. come _____

  3. in _____

  4. old _____

  5. up _____

  6. go _____

  7. hard _____

  8. smooth _____

Unit 2, Vocabulary.   Review the activities for rhyming words in Lessons 18–19, for words with like meanings in Lessons 20–21, and for words with opposite meanings in Lessons 22–23. Then read the directions with the students.

37

- **Underline the group of words that is a sentence.**

1. The Perez family needs a house.

needs a house

2. They choose this one.

They choose

3. Anthony wants

Anthony wants a new job.

4. Mr. Barker asks the questions.

asks the questions

5. Joanne calls a friend.

Joanne

6. She talks to Frank.

talks to Frank

Unit 3, Sentences. Read the directions with the students. Have students look at each photo and read the groups of words under it. Then have them underline the group of words that is a sentence.

■ **Underline the group of words that is a sentence. Then write each sentence correctly.**

1. Max walks home.   Walks Max home.

   _____

2. Plays he the radio.   He plays the radio.

   _____

3. He late is.   He is late.

   _____

4. Opens the door he.   He opens the door.

   _____

5. Max is hungry.   Is hungry Max.

   _____

6. Makes he dinner.   He makes dinner.

   _____

7. Sets the Max table.   Max sets the table.

   _____

8. The phone rings.   Rings phone the.

   _____

9. Max picks it up.   Up Max picks it.

   _____

10. No one there is.   No one is there.

   _____

11. Max down sits.   Max sits down.

   _____

Unit 3, Sentences.   Read the directions with the students. Have students read both groups of words. Ask which group makes sense. Then have them underline the group of words that makes sense. Next, have them rewrite the sentences on the lines.

39

More Word Order in Sentences

- **Write each sentence correctly.**

  1. quickly Richard jogs

  R _____

  2. cannot swim I

  I _____

  3. driving likes Pablo

  P _____

  4. a drives He truck

  H _____

  5. Mike his job likes

  M _____

  6. it at good is He

  H _____

  7. to town Eva walks

  E _____

  8. book a Ms. Fisher got

  M _____

  9. It due today is

  I _____

  10. Mr. Kim bird sees a

  M _____

  11. red It is

  I _____

  12. its There nest is

  T _____

Unit 3, Sentences. Read the directions with the students. Have students write each sentence in correct word order. The sentence must make sense.

- **Copy the telling sentences.**

Ling is **telling** her friends about her trip.
This is what she says.

1. I went to the mountains.

_____

2. I went with a friend.

_____

3. We went camping.

_____

4. We stayed in a tent.

_____

5. The weather was great.

_____

6. We stayed for one week.

_____

7. I built a campfire.

_____

8. We cooked our food over the fire.

_____

9. My friend took pictures.

_____

Unit 3, Sentences.   Read the directions with the students. Have students copy each telling sentence.

41

■ **Copy the asking sentences.**

David just met James.
He is **asking** him questions.

1. What is your name?

_____

2. What are you studying?

_____

3. Where do you live?

_____

4. How do I get there?

_____

5. What is your phone number?

_____

6. Where do you work?

_____

7. What kind of work do you do?

_____

8. Do you like your job?

_____

9. What time do you finish work?

_____

Unit 3, Sentences.   Read the directions with the students. Have students copy each asking sentence.

42

■ **Copy each sentence. Circle the number of each
asking sentence. Mark an X on the number of each
telling sentence.**

1. I got a new car.

_____

2. Do you like it?

_____

3. We can go for a drive.

_____

4. Where would you like to go?

_____

5. Will you drive me to the store?

_____

6. I can drive you to the store.

_____

7. Have you seen my keys?

_____

8. I can't find them.

_____

9. You left them in the car.

_____

10. Are you sure?

_____

11. Yes, I can see them.

_____

Unit 3, Sentences. Read the directions with the students. Have students copy each sentence. Direct
students to circle the number of each asking sentence and to put an X on the number of each telling sentence.

■ **Read each sentence. Then answer the question.**

1. Rick took his family to the zoo.

   Who did something? _____

2. The monkey did some tricks.

   What did something? _____

3. The bear ate some food.

   What did something? _____

4. The lions roared.

   What did something? _____

5. The tiger slept in its den.

   What did something? _____

6. Rick's son rode an elephant.

   Who did something? _____

7. The pink birds ran together.

   What did something? _____

8. The turtle swam in the water.

   What did something? _____

9. The owl slept in its tree.

   What did something? _____

10. Rick's daughter petted the camel.

    Who did something? _____

Unit 3, Sentences.   Read the directions with the students. Tell students that each sentence has a naming part that names someone or something. Have students read each sentence and the question below it; then have students write the answer to the question.

Sentence Parts That Show Action

■ **Read each sentence. Then answer the question.**

1. Mrs. Hanson found a dog.

What did Mrs. Hanson do? _____

2. The dog ate some food.

What did the dog do? _____

3. The dog licked Mrs. Hanson's hand.

What did the dog do? _____

4. Mrs. Hanson named the dog Skip.

What did Mrs. Hanson do? _____

5. Mrs. Hanson threw a ball.

What did Mrs. Hanson do? _____

6. Skip ran after the ball.

What did Skip do? _____

7. Skip got the ball.

What did Skip do? _____

8. Skip took a nap.

What did Skip do? _____

9. Mrs. Hanson took Skip to the vet.

What did Mrs. Hanson do? _____

10. The vet gave Skip a shot.

What did the vet do? _____

Unit 3, Sentences. Read the directions with the students. Tell students that each sentence has an action part that shows what someone or something does. Have students read each sentence and the question below it; then have students write the answer to the question.

45

- **Write each sentence using a naming part and an action part.**

ate the food.
fed the dog.
helped Dan.
wanted to run.
took a walk.

1. Dan _____

2. The dog _____

3. I _____

4. Dan and his dog _____

5. Dan's dog _____

The mice
Many people
Pat
They
She

1. _____ has two new mice.

2. _____ thinks they are very cute.

3. _____ are very small.

4. _____ are easy to keep as pets.

5. _____ don't like mice.

46

Unit 3, Sentences.   Read the directions with the students. Have students read together the first naming part and each of the action parts; then have students write the action part that makes sense. Have them continue independently. Then have students write the naming part that makes sense.

- **Underline the group of words that is a sentence.**

  1. Mr. Dawson walks Anna home.   Anna home

  2. She takes   She takes out her keys.

  3. Anna unlocks the door.   unlocks the door

  4. She waves to   She waves to Mr. Dawson.

  5. Mr. Dawson waves back.   waves back

- **Write each sentence correctly.**

  1. Mr. Dawson Anna's boss is.

  _____

  2. likes her boss Anna.

  _____

  3. He nice is.

  _____

  4. leaves Mr. Dawson.

  _____

  5. Anna into goes her house.

  _____

  6. She will him see tomorrow.

  _____

  7. dinner She starts.

  _____

  8. She eat will soon.

  _____

Unit 3, Sentences.   Review the activities for Lessons 26–28 with the students. Read the directions with the students.

47

- **Write T beside each telling sentence. Write A beside each asking sentence.**

  _____ 1. Did you go to the party?

  _____ 2. Yes, I went to the party.

  _____ 3. Were there many people at the party?

  _____ 4. There were many people there.

  _____ 5. What kind of food did they have?

  _____ 6. They had chips and dip.

  _____ 7. They also had sodas.

  _____ 8. Did you see anyone that I know?

  _____ 9. Yes, I saw many people that you know.

  _____ 10. Did you have a good time?

  _____ 11. Yes, I had a very good time.

  _____ 12. What time did the party end?

- **Combine a naming part with an action part to write a sentence.**

The woman The people The room	is very crowded. is holding a cup. are talking to each other.

  1. _____

  2. _____

  3. _____

Unit 3, Sentences. Review the activities for Lessons 29–34 with the students. Read the directions with the students.

horse truck is with eyes driver doing what cat works does where squirrel see walks a tire has and the man have in flat

- **Write three telling sentences about the photos below.**
  Use some words from the box.

1. A _____ .

2. A _____ .

3. A _____ .

- **Write three asking sentences about the photos above.**
  Use some words from the box.

1. W _____ ?

2. W _____ ?

3. W _____ ?

Unit 3, Sentences.   Read the directions with the students. Have them look at the photos. Have the students write three telling sentences, then three asking sentences using some words from the box.

- **Use the sentence parts to write a story about your life.**

The school	hope to get better jobs.
My teacher	take our books to class.
Our class	is close to my house.
My friend	go to school two times each week.
We	is full of books.
I	works hard.
Many students	helps me learn new things.
They	has many windows.
The classroom	is in the same class.
The library	go back to school.

My Life

1. _____

2. _____

3. _____

4. _____

5. _____

6. _____

7. _____

8. _____

9. _____

10. _____

Unit 3, Sentences. Read the directions with the students. Have students read the naming parts and the action parts in the boxes. Tell them to use these sentence parts to write a story about their lives. Have students read their stories aloud to the class.

Lesson 35

Naming Words

- **Write the correct naming word under each photo.**

1. woman

man

family

_____   _____   _____

2. city

house

store

_____   _____   _____

3. apple

car

fish

_____   _____   _____

4. book

watch

clock

_____   _____   _____

Unit 4, Grammar and Usage.   Read the directions with the students. Tell students that some words are naming words and that naming words can name people, places, or things. Then have them read each group of naming words and write the correct word under each photo.

51

- **Read the sentences. Circle the special naming words.**

1. The <u>man</u> is (Pat).
2. The <u>woman</u> is Mary.
3. The <u>baby</u> is Sara.
4. My <u>son</u> is Tony.
5. My <u>daughter</u> is Ann.

6. My <u>sister</u> is Lee Chin.
7. My <u>brother</u> is Scott.
8. My <u>friend</u> is Ms. Alba.
9. Our <u>neighbor</u> is Mr. Ross.
10. My <u>doctor</u> is Dr. Brown.

- **List the naming words and the special naming words from the sentences shown above.**

People
1. man
2.
3.
4.
5.
6.
7.
8.
9.
10.

Special Names
1. Pat
2.
3.
4.
5.
6.
7.
8.
9.
10.

Unit 4, Grammar and Usage. Read the directions with the students. Explain that people have special names. Have students read the underlined word, then circle the special naming word. Have them write each naming word in the correct column. Tell them that special naming words begin with capital letters.

More Naming Words

- **Read the story. Circle the special place names.**

Where I Live

1. The <u>city</u> I live in is (Kansas City).

2. The <u>street</u> I live on is First Street.

3. My <u>office</u> is at The Rental Place.

4. The <u>park</u> I walk in is Peace Park.

5. The <u>beach</u> I swim at is Sun Beach.

6. The <u>library</u> I go to is Elm Library.

7. The <u>store</u> I shop in is City Books.

8. The <u>bank</u> I use is the Bank of Missouri.

9. The <u>hospital</u> I live near is Memorial Hospital.

10. My <u>apartment</u> is in the Parkview Apartments.

- **List the naming words and the special place names from the sentences shown above.**

Places	Special Places
1. city	1. Kansas City
2.	2.
3.	3.
4.	4.
5.	5.
6.	6.
7.	7.
8.	8.
9.	9.
10.	10.

Unit 4, Grammar and Usage. Read the directions with the students. Explain that many places have special names. Have them read the underlined word in each sentence, then circle the special naming word. Have them write each naming word in the correct column.

■ **Write the word that means more than one.**

1. one radio

three <u>radios</u>

4. one nest

two _____

2. one pencil

four _____

5. one dog

five _____

3. one book

six _____

6. one fork

ten _____

■ **Write the word that best completes each sentence.**

1. I use my _____ to walk.
(leg, legs)

2. I use my _____ to think.
(head, heads)

3. I use my _____ to hear.
(ear, ears)

4. I use my _____ to see.
(eye, eyes)

5. I use my _____ to smell.
(nose, noses)

Unit 4, Grammar and Usage. Read the directions with the students. Have them look at the first photo and read *one radio*. Then have students read *three radios*. Tell them to add *-s* to make the naming words in Exercises 2–6 mean more than one. Have them read the sentences and fill in the missing words.

- **Look at the photos. Then use an action word from the box to tell about each photo.**

| paint | jog | eat | cheer | grow | talk | meet | shop |

1. workers _____

2. flowers _____

3. men _____

4. friends _____

5. fans _____

6. people _____

7. runners _____

8. students _____

Unit 4, Grammar and Usage.   Read the directions with the students. Tell students that action words tell what people or things do. Have students choose a word from the box to tell what is happening in each photo, then write the word on the lines.

■ **Write the action word from the box that best completes each sentence.**

| go | asks | need | sells | talk | writes |

1. Brad and Julie _____ a new washer.

2. They _____ to the store.

3. They _____ to a woman there about washers.

4. Brad _____ the woman some questions.

5. The woman _____ Brad and Julie a washer.

6. Julie _____ a check.

■ **Write the action word from the box that best completes each sentence.**

| likes | learn | help | takes | holds | looks |

1. George _____ to listen to guitar music.

2. He _____ guitar lessons each week.

3. The lessons help George _____ how to play.

4. Mr. Carlson can _____ his son practice.

5. He _____ the music for George.

6. George _____ at the music on the paper.

Unit 4, Grammar and Usage.   Read the directions with the students. Have students read the action words in the box at the top of the page. Then have them read each sentence, choose the word that makes sense, and write it on the line. Follow the same procedure at the bottom of the page.

- **Underline the action words. Circle the -s on the action words.**

1. The woman work(s).

   The women work.

2. The dog jumps.

   The dogs jump.

3. The doorbell rings.

   The doorbells ring.

4. The clock works well.

   The clocks work well.

5. The man walks slowly.

   The men walk slowly.

6. The car honks.

   The cars honk.

7. The horse runs fast.

   The horses run fast.

8. The plant grows quickly.

   The plants grow quickly.

- **Use action words from the box to complete the sentences.**

| rolls | blows | writes | thinks | works |
| roll | blow | write | think | work |

1. The stoves _____ well.

   The stove _____ well.

2. The fan _____ cool air.

   The fans _____ cool air.

3. The orange _____ away.

   The oranges _____ away.

4. My friends _____ me a letter.

   My friend _____ me a letter.

5. The student _____ carefully.

   The students _____ carefully.

Unit 4, Grammar and Usage.   Read the directions with the students. Have them read the first set of sentences and discuss the differences in the action words. Have them underline the action words in sentences 2–8, circle each -s, and complete the second group of sentences with words from the box.

57

■ **Write the word that best completes each sentence.**

1. Today Hoan _____ the piano.
(play, plays)

He _____ a new song.
(learn, learns)

2. Today Sue _____ to the park.
(walk, walks)

She _____ up the steps.
(climb, climbs)

3. Today Rosa _____ into the lake.
(jump, jumps)

She _____ in the water.
(walk, walks)

4. Today Ray _____ to the pond.
(jog, jogs)

He _____ to his friend there.
(talk, talks)

5. Amanda _____ computers.
(fix, fixes)

She _____ her job.
(enjoy, enjoys)

6. Calvin _____ every day for the race.
(train, trains)

He _____ to win first place.
(hope, hopes)

7. Jamie _____ at a day-care center.
(work, works)

She _____ children.
(like, likes)

Unit 4, Grammar and Usage. Read the directions with the students. Tell students that *-s* is added to most action words to tell what one person or thing does today. Have them read each sentence and write the correct action word on the lines.

■ **Write the word that best completes each sentence.**

1. Yesterday Hoan _____ the piano.

(play, played)

   He _____ a new song.

(learn, learned)

2. Yesterday Sue _____ to the park.

(walk, walked)

   She _____ up the steps.

(climb, climbed)

3. Yesterday Rosa _____ into the lake.

(jump, jumped)

   She _____ in the water.

(walk, walked)

4. Yesterday Ray _____ to the pond.

(jog, jogged)

   He _____ to his friend there.

(talk, talked)

5. Amanda _____ computers.

(fix, fixed)

   She _____ her job.

(enjoy, enjoyed)

6. Calvin _____ every day for the race.

(train, trained)

   He _____ to win first place.

(hope, hoped)

7. Jamie _____ at a day-care center.

(work, worked)

   She _____ children.

(like, liked)

Unit 4, Grammar and Usage. Read the directions with the students. Tell students that *-ed* is added to most action words to tell what happened in the past. Have them read each sentence and write the correct action word on the lines.

59

- **Write is or are to complete each sentence.**

1. It _____ summer.

2. It _____ warm outside.

3. The Johnsons _____ going on a trip.

4. They _____ going to the Grand Canyon.

5. The family _____ leaving today.

6. Mr. Johnson _____ packing the car.

7. He _____ taking a map for the trip.

8. The children _____ excited.

9. They _____ helping to pack the car.

10. Mrs. Johnson _____ making a picnic lunch.

11. The family _____ going to stop at the lake.

12. They _____ going to have a picnic there.

13. Everyone _____ ready to go.

14. The Johnsons _____ on their way.

15. They _____ all happy to get to the lake.

16. Everyone _____ enjoying the picnic lunch.

17. Now they _____ on their way again.

18. They _____ ready to see the Grand Canyon!

60

Unit 4, Grammar and Usage. Read the directions with the students. Tell students to use *is* when they speak of one person or thing in the present and to use *are* when they speak of more than one person or thing in the present. Have them read each sentence and write *is* or *are* on the lines.

Using *Was* or *Were*

- **Use <u>was</u> or <u>were</u> to complete each sentence.**

1. I _____ at the park.

2. My dog _____ at the park.

3. We _____ at the park together.

4. My dog and I _____ going to walk around the park.

5. Then I _____ going to play softball.

6. My friend _____ at the park, too.

7. His arm _____ in a cast.

8. He _____ not going to play.

9. He _____ going to hold my dog.

10. Both teams _____ on the field.

11. The fans _____ cheering for their teams.

12. The teams _____ playing well.

13. The game _____ fun.

14. It _____ a great day!

15. The game _____ close.

16. The score _____ tied.

17. But our team _____ the winner.

18. We _____ all very happy!

Unit 4, Grammar and Usage. Read the directions with the students. Tell students to use *was* when they speak of one person or thing in the past and to use *were* when they speak of more than one person or thing in the past. Have them read each sentence and write *was* or *were* on the lines.

▪ **Circle the word that best completes each sentence.**

1. I (see, saw) a TV show now.

2. Yesterday Ann (see, saw) a TV show.

3. Now Kim and Ann (see, saw) the same TV show.

4. Last night Kim (ran, run) to the store.

5. She (see, saw) some friends there.

6. Now I (ran, run) to the store.

7. As I leave the store, I (ran, run) into a friend of mine.

8. Yesterday Ann (ran, run) home from work.

9. Now Kim and Ann (ran, run) to the park.

10. Now I (come, came) to the park.

11. Yesterday Kim and Ann (come, came) to my house.

12. Now they (come, came) again.

▪ **Rewrite the sentences using the correct word.**

1. I __ (see, saw) a pretty picture now.

   _____

2. Last night Kim __ (ran, run) fast.

   _____

3. Then she __ (come, came) to see me.

   _____

Unit 4, Grammar and Usage.   Tell students to use *see*, *come*, and *run* to tell something that happens today and to use *saw*, *came*, and *ran* to tell something that happened in the past. Then read the directions and sentences with students.

Jan writes
She writes.

Ron reads
He reads.

■ **Rewrite the sentence using she or he.**

1. Jan has a pencil.

She

2. Ron has a book.

3. Jan writes with the pencil.

4. Ron reads the book.

5. Jan enjoys writing stories.

6. Ron likes to read stories.

7. Ron finishes the book.

Unit 4, Grammar and Usage. Read the directions with the students. Have them read the sentences at the top of the page and note which words are used in place of the names. Have them read the first sentence and substitute the word *she* for the name. Have them rewrite all the sentences in the same way.

63

Tom and I will run the race.
We will run the race.

Pat and Bill will run the race.
They will run the race.

- **Rewrite the sentences using <u>we</u> or <u>they</u>.**

1. Tom and I are here.

   We _____

2. Pat and Bill are not here yet.

   They _____

3. Pat and Bill are late.

   _____

4. Pat and Bill might miss the race.

   _____

5. Tom and I are on time.

   _____

6. Tom and I will be in the race.

   _____

7. Pat and Bill get there just in time.

   _____

Unit 4, Grammar and Usage.   Read the directions with the students. Have them read the sentences at the top of the page and note which words are used in place of the names. Have them read the first sentence and substitute the word *we* for the names. Have them rewrite all the sentences in the same way.

I see you.

Derrick and I see you.

- **Write I to complete each sentence.**

1. Jim and _____ go to the pond.

2. The park is not far from where _____ live.

3. Jim and _____ go there to fish.

4. Jim and _____ always have a good time there.

5. _____ sit on the grass.

6. _____ sit by Jim.

7. _____ take out my fishing rod.

8. _____ help Jim put a worm on his hook.

9. Jim and _____ catch fish.

10. _____ look at the water.

11. _____ can see some other fish.

12. Jim and _____ have fun.

13. _____ caught four fish.

14. Jim and _____ caught ten fish in all.

15. _____ put the fish in a bucket.

Unit 4, Grammar and Usage.   Read the directions with the students. Have students read the two examples of the proper use of *I*. Then have students add *I* to each sentence.

a b c d e f g h i j k l m
n o p q r s t u v w x y z

- **Write the names of the vowels.**

1. The vowels are _____ , _____ , _____ , _____ , _____ .

- **Write *an* if it would be used before each word.**

1. _____ olive

2. _____ ace

3. _____ egg

4. _____ elbow

- **Write *an* if it would be used before each word.**

1. _____ apron

2. _____ ocean

3. _____ folder

4. _____ aunt

5. _____ candle

6. _____ uncle

7. _____ area

8. _____ box

9. _____ job

- **Write *an* if it would be used before each group of words.**

1. _____ baby bottle

2. _____ animal shop

3. _____ toy truck

4. _____ oak tree

5. _____ barnyard

6. _____ ice cream cone

Unit 4, Grammar and Usage.   Read the directions with the students. Have them say the alphabet and write the shaded letters called vowels. Tell them that *an* is used before words that begin with a vowel. Then have them read each word or group of words and write *an* only in front of the appropriate ones.

- **Circle the consonants.**

a b c d e f g h i j k l m
n o p q r s t u v w x y z

- **Write a or an before each word.**

1. _____ train
   (a, an)

2. _____ tent
   (a, an)

3. _____ bug
   (a, an)

4. _____ bike
   (a, an)

5. _____ ant
   (a, an)

6. _____ uncle
   (a, an)

7. _____ van
   (a, an)

8. _____ ship
   (a, an)

- **Complete the sentences with a or an and a naming word.**

1. I saw _a movie_____.

2. I can ride on _____.

3. I go to _____.

4. I know about _____.

5. I work for _____.

6. I need _____.

7. I like _____.

8. I don't like _____.

Unit 4, Grammar and Usage.   Read the directions with the students. Have them say the alphabet and circle the consonants. Tell them that *a* is used before words that begin with a consonant. Have them read each word and write *a* or *an* on the lines. Have them complete the sentences using phrases with *a* or *an*.

■ **Circle the word that describes each photo.**

1. 	clean noisy quiet	4. 	wide lazy hungry
2. 	sad happy mad	5. 	cold fast long
3.	big shiny flat	6.	mad friendly busy

■ **Complete each sentence using the words you circled above.**

1. The city is _____ noisy _____ .

2. The woman is _____ .

3. The toaster is _____ .

4. The family is _____ .

5. The ice is _____ .

6. Dan's boss is _____ .

Unit 4, Grammar and Usage.   Read the directions with the students. Have them identify the photos and read the words together. Have them circle one word in each box that tells how the thing or person looks or feels. Have students write the correct circled word in each sentence at the bottom of the page.

■ **Read about each photo. Then circle the words that answer each question.**

1. Sandra likes her big old dog.
   He is black, brown, and white.
   His hair is soft.

   Which words tell about Sandra's dog?

red	white	old	big
brown	black	soft	wet

2. The large, heavy truck is white.
   It is empty right now.

   Which words tell about the truck?

light	white	full	black
empty	little	heavy	large

3. Joe lost his old brown helmet.
   Then he got a new red helmet.

   Which words tell about Joe's
   new helmet?

old	brown	blue	lost
new	clean	red	tall

4. This shiny, red apple is sweet.
   It tastes good.

   Which words tell about the apple?

clean	good	short	red
shiny	pretty	soft	sweet

Unit 4, Grammar and Usage. Read the directions with the students. Have students read each story together. Then have them circle the words that answer each question.

- **Underline the naming words in each sentence.**

    1. Miss Taylor drove the young children to the circus.

    2. The large elephants walked into a brown tent.

- **Circle the action word in each sentence.**

    1. The children watched the elephants.

    2. Everyone laughed at the clowns.

- **Draw a box around the describing words in each sentence.**

    1. The funny clown kicked his big feet.

    2. The happy children clapped their small hands.

- **Circle the special naming word in each sentence. Then write the naming word and the special naming word in the correct columns.**

    1. The dog is named Pepi.

    2. The cat is named Leo.

    3. My horse is called Blaze.

    4. Is your fish named Flipper?

Animals	Special Names
1. _____	1. _____
2. _____	2. _____
3. _____	3. _____
4. _____	4. _____

- **Write the word that means more than one.**

  1. one car

  six _____

  2. one banana

  two _____

  3. one desk

  four _____

  4. one book

  five _____

- **Write the word that best completes each sentence.**

  1. We _____ in school.   (is, are)

  2. My friend _____ here.   (is, are)

  3. Did you _____ my books?   (see, saw)

  4. Yes, I _____ your books yesterday.   (see, saw)

  5. Your books _____ on the table.   (is, are)

  6. I _____ sitting at that table.   (was, were)

  7. _____ you going home after school?   (Is, Are)

  8. After school I will _____ to the store.   (run, ran)

- **Draw a line to match each word with the correct pronoun.**

  1. John   she

  2. Sue   he

  3. Sue and John   we

  4. Bill and I   they

Unit 4, Grammar and Usage.   Review the activities for one and more than one in Lesson 38, for using the correct action words in Lessons 44–46, and for using *she, he, we,* and *they* in Lessons 47–48. Then read the directions with the students.

71

Using What You've Learned

- **Write the word that best completes each sentence.**

1. Tim and Janet _____ in the park.   (is, are)

2. Tim _____ very quickly.   (walk, walks)

3. Janet _____ slower than Tim.   (walk, walks)

4. Tim and Janet _____ in the yard yesterday.   (work, worked)

5. Tim _____ weeds.   (pull, pulled)

6. Janet _____ some seeds.   (plant, planted)

7. Tim _____ the seeds.   (water, watered)

8. Janet and Tim _____ tired after working all day.   (was, were)

- **Copy the sentences shown above. Use He, She, or They in place of the underlined names.**

1. _____

2. _____

3. _____

4. _____

5. _____

6. _____

7. _____

8. _____

Unit 4, Grammar and Usage.   Read the directions with the students.

72

- **Write the word that best completes each sentence.**

The Office Building

1. The office building _____ tall.
   (is, are)

   It is _____ large building.
   (a, an)

2. The building has _____ elevator.
   (a, an)

   It is _____ fast elevator.
   (a, an)

3. James _____ in the elevator.
   (is, are)

   _____ is going to work.
   (She, He)

4. The people _____ hard.
   (work, works)

   _____ get up early every morning.
   (We, They)

5. Many people _____ near the office building.
   (live, lives)

   They _____ to work.
   (walk, walks)

6. Carol _____ a bike to work.
   (ride, rides)

   _____ parks it by the door.
   (She, He)

Unit 4, Grammar and Usage.   Read the directions with the students.

73

- **Read the sentences. Underline the capital letter at the beginning of each sentence.**

1. Mark needs a new radio.

2. There are so many radios.

3. Which one is best?

4. It is hard to choose.

5. Mark sees one he likes.

6. He turns it on and listens to it.

7. It sounds great!

8. How much does it cost?

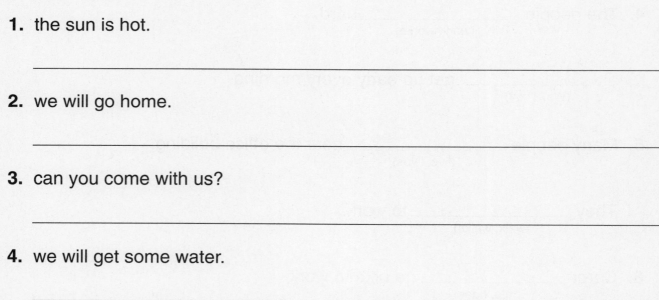

- **Rewrite the sentences. Begin each sentence with a capital letter.**

1. the sun is hot.

   _____

2. we will go home.

   _____

3. can you come with us?

   _____

4. we will get some water.

   _____

5. what time is it?

   _____

Unit 5, Capitalization and Punctuation. Read the directions with the students. Tell them that a sentence always begins with a capital letter. Have them read the first eight sentences and underline the first letter of each. Then have them rewrite the sentences at the bottom of the page correctly.

Writing Names of People

- **Read the names of these people. Underline the capital letter that begins each name. Then write the names.**

Josie

Mr. Collins

1. _____   **2.** _____

- **Rewrite the names. Begin each name with a capital letter.**

1. pat long _____

2. eva ramos _____

3. bill adams _____

4. will brown _____

5. mr. franklin _____

6. mrs. douglas _____

7. ms. baxter _____

8. dr. butala _____

Unit 5, Capitalization and Punctuation. Read the directions with the students. Tell them that names of people always begin with a capital letter. Have students underline the capital letters that begin the first two names, then rewrite them. Then have them rewrite the names at the bottom of the page correctly.

75

■ **Name each pet using the words in the box. Begin each pet name with a capital letter.**

chip	tiger	king	jet	goldy	speedy

1. _____

4. _____

2. _____

5. _____

3. _____

6. _____

Unit 5, Capitalization and Punctuation.   Read the directions with the students. Tell students that names for animals also begin with capital letters. Have them name each pet, using the words in the box. Then have them rewrite each name with a capital letter.

| Sunday | Monday | Tuesday | Wednesday |
| Thursday | | Friday | Saturday |

- **Use the names of the days in the box above to answer the questions. Begin the name of each day with a capital letter.**

1. What day comes before Tuesday?

   _____

2. What day comes after Thursday?

   _____

3. What day comes after Saturday?

   _____

4. What day comes before Wednesday?

   _____

5. What two days start with the letter T?

   _____   _____

6. What two days start with the letter S?

   _____   _____

7. What day begins with W?

   _____

8. What are the last two days of the week?

   _____   _____

Unit 5, Capitalization and Punctuation.   Read the directions with the students. Tell them that the name of each day begins with a capital letter. Have students read the list of days. Discuss the meanings of the words *before, after,* and *last.* Then have them answer the questions.

Writing Names of Months

- **Rewrite the names of the months. Begin the name of each month with a capital letter.**

1. january

_____

7. july

_____

2. february

_____

8. august

_____

3. march

_____

9. september

_____

4. april

_____

10. october

_____

5. may

_____

11. november

_____

6. june

_____

12. december

_____

Unit 5, Capitalization and Punctuation. Read the directions with the students. Tell them that the name of each month begins with a capital letter. Have students read the names of the months. Then have them rewrite the names, capitalizing each one.

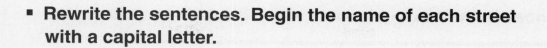
- **Rewrite the sentences. Begin the name of each street with a capital letter.**

   1. Bob lives on jones street.

   _____

   2. He works on river road.

   _____

   3. I live on oak street.

   _____

   4. I work on lake drive.

   _____

   5. My bank is on first street.

   _____

- **Rewrite the sentences. Begin the name of each city with a capital letter.**

   1. Diane lives in dallas.

   _____

   2. She came from paris.

   _____

   3. My home is in montreal.

   _____

   4. My friend lives in boston.

   _____

   5. Have you ever been to kansas city?

   _____

Unit 5, Capitalization and Punctuation.   Read the directions with the students. Tell them that names of places, such as cities and streets, begin with a capital letter. Have them read the first five sentences and rewrite them using capital letters where needed. Repeat with city names.

79

- **Read the sentences in the box.**

I am a man.	My friend and I like to play tennis.
I am a woman.	My friend and I like to read.
I am at home.	My friend and I jog each day.
I am not at home.	My friend and I like to talk.
I do not have a pet.	My friend and I like to go bowling.
I have a pet.	My friend and I work together.
I feed my pet.	My friend and I go to movies.
I have a family.	My friend and I study together.

- **Use ten sentences from the box to write about yourself.**

1. _____
2. _____
3. _____
4. _____
5. _____
6. _____
7. _____
8. _____
9. _____
10. _____

Unit 5, Capitalization and Punctuation.   Read the directions with the students. Tell them that the word *I* is always written with a capital letter. Have the students read the sentences at the top of the page. Then have them choose ten of the sentences to write a story about themselves.

Lesson 61

- **Put a period at the end of each telling sentence.**

1. Lisa looks at the photos

2. She keeps them in a book

3. The photos are of Lisa's family

4. Some of the photos are old

5. Other photos are new

6. Lisa puts new photos in the book every year

7. The photos are special to Lisa

- **Rewrite each sentence, and end it with a period.**

1. This is my home

   _____

2. I cut the grass

   _____

3. Next, I rake it

   _____

4. Then I pull the weeds

   _____

5. It looks good

   _____

6. I put my tools away

   _____

Unit 5, Capitalization and Punctuation. Read the directions with the students. Tell students that telling sentences always end with a period. Have them read each telling sentence at the top of the page and put a period at the end. Then have them rewrite each sentence at the bottom of the page correctly.

- **Put a question mark at the end of each asking sentence.**

1. Will I get that new job

2. When will I find out about it

3. Who will call me

4. Should I call to ask about the job

5. What will my new job be like

6. What will my new office look like

7. How much money will I make

- **Rewrite each sentence, and end it with a question mark.**

1. Who said my name

   _____

2. Was it Bud

   _____

3. Did Bud go home

   _____

4. When will he come back

   _____

5. Isn't his car broken down

   _____

6. How did he get home

   _____

Unit 5, Capitalization and Punctuation.   Read the directions with the students. Tell them that asking sentences end with a question mark. Have students read each asking sentence at the top of the page and put a question mark at the end. Then have them rewrite each sentence at the bottom of the page correctly.

Lesson
63

Ending Sentences

■ **Read the sentences. End each sentence with a period or a question mark. Then rewrite each sentence correctly.**

1. Our town often floods

_____

2. The river gets too full

_____

3. Will the river flood today

_____

4. It floods whenever it rains

_____

5. How can we stop the floods

_____

6. Should we build a dam

_____

7. A dam will help stop the floods

_____

8. How long will it take to build the dam

_____

9. It will take one year to build

_____

Unit 5, Capitalization and Punctuation. Read the directions with the students. Have them read the sentences. Tell students to put a period at the end of each telling sentence and a question mark at the end of each asking sentence.

83

January 1, 1994	July 4, 1993

- **Circle the date in each sentence. Rewrite each date correctly on the lines.**

1. I got a valentine on february 14 1994.

_____

2. Jan had a New Year's party on january 1 1993.

_____

3. I went to a costume party on october 31 1991.

_____

4. Leo ate turkey on november 23 1993.

_____

5. My birthday party was on july 4 1993.

_____

6. Greg left for his summer vacation on august 9 1994.

_____

7. I wrote you a letter on april 12 1994.

_____

8. You wrote back on may 5 1994.

_____

9. Today is ___ .

_____

Unit 5, Capitalization and Punctuation. Read the directions with the students. Tell them that a comma means to pause, then read on. Have them read the dates in the box. Point out the capital letters. Tell them a comma is used to separate the day from the year. Have them circle each date, then write it correctly.

■ Put a period or a question mark at the end of each sentence. Rewrite the sentences. Use capital letters where needed.

1. joe garza and i ride to work together

_____

2. we will be off on friday

_____

3. did joe call his brother, ray

_____

4. last friday i called ray

_____

5. do you work on monday

_____

6. i work on monday

_____

7. ray will visit in september

_____

8. he is coming from toronto

_____

9. how long will he stay

_____

Unit 5, Capitalization and Punctuation. Read the directions with the students. Have students read the sentences. Have them add a period or a question mark to each. Then have them rewrite the sentences, using capital letters where needed.

85

- **Rewrite each sentence correctly.**

   1. i saw sue

   _____

   2. she lives on lee road

   _____

   3. she was born may 1 1958

   _____

   4. her dog is named wags

   _____

   5. wags is a friendly dog

   _____

   6. sue is a doctor

   _____

   7. her office is on first street

   _____

   8. she is a good doctor

   _____

   9. many people visit her

   _____

   10. sue is always busy

   _____

Unit 5, Capitalization and Punctuation. Read the directions with the students. Have the students rewrite the sentences correctly.

- **Write the information that completes each sentence. Use capital letters and commas where needed.**

1. My name is ___ .

_____

2. My street is ___ .

_____

3. My city is ___ .

_____

4. My country is ___ .

_____

5. My company is ___ .

_____

6. The street my office is on is ___ .

_____

7. My boss is ___ .

_____

8. I work with ___ .

_____

9. My birthday is ___ .

_____

10. Today's date is ___ .

_____

Unit 5, Capitalization and Punctuation. Read the directions with the students. Have students write the information that completes each sentence. Remind students to use capital letters and commas where needed.

87

- **Read the sentences in the box.**

1. where is bill	8. what is he making
2. he is in the house	9. the snack is sweet
3. he just got home	10. it is a good snack
4. bill has two cookies	11. would you like some
5. what is bill doing	12. yes, i would
6. he is making a snack	13. this is really good
7. can he cook	

- **Write each sentence in the box correctly on the lines.**

1. _____

2. _____

3. _____

4. _____

5. _____

6. _____

7. _____

8. _____

9. _____

10. _____

11. _____

12. _____

13. _____

Unit 5, Capitalization and Punctuation.   Read the directions with the students. Have them read each sentence at the top of the page. Have the students rewrite the sentences on the lines, using capital letters and punctuation where needed.

flowers	day	friend
garden	rain	seeds
store	sun	table
weeds	basket	vegetables
soup	plants	neighbor

- **Choose naming words from the box to complete each sentence.**

1. Sandra went to the _____ .

2. She got some little brown _____ .

3. Sandra will plant the seeds in the _____ .

4. She will check the garden every _____ .

5. Sandra will pull the _____ from the garden.

6. The _____ will fall on the garden.

7. The _____ will warm the garden.

8. Pretty _____ will grow in the garden.

9. Many _____ will also grow in the garden.

10. Sandra will put the vegetables in a _____ .

11. She will use the vegetables to make _____ .

12. She will give some of the soup to her _____ .

13. Sandra will give some of the flowers to a _____ .

14. Her friend will put them in a vase on a _____ .

15. Her friend really likes flowers and _____ .

Unit 6, Composition. Read the directions with the students. Have students choose naming words from the box to complete each sentence.

needs	live	find
shop	cut	lifts
write	read	take
opens	ask	likes
chooses	buy	want

■ **Choose action words from the box to complete each sentence.**

1. Pat and Carmen _____ together.

2. They _____ at the store every week.

3. They _____ all of the ads in the newspaper.

4. They _____ some coupons they can use.

5. They _____ the coupons out with scissors.

6. Then Pat _____ the cabinet.

7. Pat _____ to know what they should buy.

8. Carmen _____ a can to see the label.

9. They _____ a list.

10. They _____ the list and the coupons to the store.

11. They _____ the butcher for some ground beef.

12. Pat _____ fresh fruit.

13. They _____ some lettuce and tomatoes.

14. They _____ salad for dinner.

15. Carmen _____ chicken to have with the salad.

Unit 6, Composition. Read the directions with the students. Have students choose action words from the box to complete each sentence.

Are you standing or sitting?

I am sitting.

- **Write a complete sentence to answer each question.**

1. Are you a man or a woman?

_____

2. Are you working or relaxing?

_____

3. Do you use a pen or a pencil?

_____

4. Do you walk or drive to work?

_____

5. Do you like grapes or raisins?

_____

6. Do you live in a house or an apartment?

_____

7. Do you cook or go out to eat?

_____

8. Do you watch TV or read books?

_____

Unit 6, Composition.   Read the directions with the students. Discuss the example with the students.
Then have students read the questions and write each answer as a complete sentence.

91

Writing More Sentences

- **Draw lines to match the sentence parts. Then write the sentences on the lines below.**

Naming	**Action**
My phone	honk.
The water	breaks.
The door	barks.
Those cars	cries.
A dish	splashes.
The scissors	cut.
Our dog	slams.
The baby	rings.

1. My _____
   Naming   Action

2. _____
   Naming   Action

3. _____
   Naming   Action

4. _____
   Naming   Action

5. _____
   Naming   Action

6. _____
   Naming   Action

7. _____
   Naming   Action

8. _____
   Naming   Action

Unit 6, Composition. Read the directions with the students. Have students draw lines to match the sentence parts. Then have them write the sentences on the lines below.

A Thank-You Letter

■ **Study this thank-you letter.**

June 6, 1994 ◄—— date

greeting ——► Dear Janet,

 Thank you for asking me to your dinner ◄
party. I had a very good time. ◄ ├— body

 Your friend, ◄—— closing
 Lisa

■ **Rewrite the greetings. Use commas as shown.**

1. Dear Janet, _____

2. Dear Mother, _____

3. Dear Tom, _____

4. Dear Ms. Roberts, _____

5. Dear Mr. Chang, _____

■ **Rewrite the closings. Use commas as shown.**

1. Your friend, _____

 (your name) _____

2. Love, _____

 Aaron _____

3. Sincerely, _____

 Michelle _____

4. Yours truly, _____

 Dawn _____

Unit 6, Composition. Read the directions with the students. Read and discuss the parts of the letter.
Then have students rewrite the greetings and closings. Remind them to use commas as shown.

93

- **Read the thank-you letter below.**

> May 1, 1994
>
> Dear Mr. Green,
>   Thank you for the book you sent to me about recycling. It was very helpful and interesting. Please send me one of your new catalogs.
>   Yours truly,
>   Anthony Perez

- **Now write the thank-you letter on the lines.**

Dear _____

_____

_____

_____

_____

_____

_____

_____

94

Unit 6, Composition.   Read the directions with the students. Have students read the thank-you letter, and write the letter on the lines.

■ **Read the poem. Circle the words that rhyme.**

Your birthday is near.

Yes, it's that time of year.

Stand tall, be bold.

Don't say that you're old.

Just have a great day.

What more can I say?

■ **Read each poem. Circle the correct rhyming words.**

We got on a ship

We took a long ___ .

   (time, trip, jump)

Our trip had been fun.

But now it was ___ .

   (larger, sad, done)

It's the team's lucky day.

They are ready, willing, and able to ___ .

   (eat, sleep, play)

The fans yell a cheer.

That's all you can ___ .

   (see, hear, taste)

Unit 6, Composition.   Read the directions with the students. Remind students that some words rhyme. Read the first poem together, and have them circle the rhyming words. Then have them read the other poems and circle the correct rhyming word.

▪ **Choose a word from the box to complete each sentence.**

letters	trip	drove	write	visited	play

1. Do you like to get _____ ?

2. Let's _____ a letter.

3. We can tell about our _____ .

4. We _____ to Miami, Florida.

5. We _____ a museum there.

6. We also saw a _____ there.

▪ **Use complete sentences to answer the questions.**

1. Do you like chocolate or vanilla ice cream?

   _____

2. Is it sunny or rainy today?

   _____

3. Do you like to read stories or poems?

   _____

4. Do you live close to or far away from your job?

   _____

5. Do you like football or baseball?

   _____

6. Are you tall or short?

   _____

Unit 6, Composition. Read the directions with the students. Have students choose a word from the box to complete each sentence at the top of the page. Then have students answer the questions using complete sentences.

- **Label the parts of the letter below. Write the letter of the correct choice from the box.**

A. Body	B. Closing	C. Date	D. Greeting

May 7, 1994   **1.** _____

2. _____ Dear Kevin,

Thank you for taking me to work last week.

3. _____ I really needed a ride. I will take you to work next week.

Sincerely,   **4.** _____

Kendra

- **Draw lines to match the words that rhyme.**

1.	cab	sock
2.	bank	well
3.	clock	mug
4.	stuck	cheap
5.	week	fill
6.	sell	dice
7.	sleep	truck
8.	price	grab
9.	spill	speak
10.	rug	drank

Unit 6, Composition.   Read the directions with the students. At the top of the page, have students label the parts of the letter. Then have students draw lines to match the words that rhyme.

97

- **Use a word from the first box to fill the first blank in each sentence. Use a word from the second box to fill the second blank in each sentence.**

boss	women
friends	football
men	sun
dog	park
people	cars

leaves	walk
barks	jog
talk	stop
play	closes
meet	rolls

1. The _____ _____ at five o'clock.

2. The _____ _____ out the door.

3. Three _____ _____ in the park.

4. The amusement _____ _____ at six o'clock.

5. The _____ _____ at the cat in a tree.

6. Two _____ _____ about work.

7. Four _____ _____ at the fountain.

8. My _____ _____ the same time I do.

- **Now write four sentences of your own.**

1. _____

2. _____

3. _____

4. _____

Unit 6, Composition. Read the directions with the students. Have students complete each sentence using a word from the box on the left in the first blank and a word from the box on the right in the second blank. Then have them write sentences of their own, using naming words and action words.

- **Read the letter. Write the letter on the lines below.**

1. May 5, 1994
2. Dear Mr. Jefferson,
3.   Thank you for talking to me about the clinic I would like to open. You have given me some good ideas. Our town needs a clinic to help sick people. I would like to start building it as soon as possible.
4. Sincerely,
   Dr. Sharon Turner

Unit 6, Composition. Read the directions with the students. Read the parts of the letter together. Have students write the letter on the lines, using the current year.

99

Finding the Ones That Are Alike ▪ Circle the things that are alike in some way. In row 1, mark an X on the photo to the right of the basketball. In row 2, mark an X on the photo to the left of the milk.

1.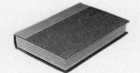

2.

Finding the One That Is Different ▪ Mark an X on the photo that is different.

1.

Adding Missing Parts ▪ Circle each photo that has a missing part. Then draw the missing part.

1.   2.

Reversals ▪ Mark an X on the photo that is facing a different way.

1.    2.

Study Skills.   Read the directions with the students.

Remembering the Order ▪ Read the story. Then number the photos in the correct order.

1.   Carmen and Ricardo want to cook dinner. First, Carmen goes to the store. Then she brings the food home. Ricardo helps her carry the bags. Finally, they cook their dinner.

_____   _____   _____

Missing Letters ▪ Write the missing letters.

1. A _____ C

2. J K _____

3. _____ Q R

4. f g _____

5. m _____ o

6. _____ x y

Alphabetical Order ▪ Write the words in alphabetical order.

1. Diane   _____

Maria   _____

Ling   _____

2. rain   _____

woman   _____

car   _____

3. house _____

man _____

fly _____

4. truck _____

lake _____

zoo _____

Listening to Sounds ▪ Mark an X on the photo that answers each question.

1. Which do you hear when you wake up?

3. Which do you hear when you are watching your favorite show?

2. Which do you hear when you want to cool off?

4. Which do you hear when you fill up your car or truck with gas?

Rhyming Words ▪ Read each sentence. Circle the words that rhyme.

1. Pat sat on the mat.

2. A bug is on the rug.

3. The frog will hop on the mop.

4. The brown bear ate a pear.

5. A bee is in the tree.

6. I have fun when I'm in the sun.

7. Jim needs more light to see at night.

8. Sue saw her coat on the boat.

9. Joan likes to wait by the gate.

10. Is there a mouse in Tony's house?

Vocabulary.   Read the directions with the students.

Like Meanings ▪ Circle the words that mean almost the same.

1. dark large big

2. go leave come

3. print sing write

4. high short tall

5. end start begin

6. small old little

Opposite Meanings ▪ Circle the word that means the opposite of the underlined word in each sentence.

1. Please <u>close</u> the door.   (shut, open)

2. It is very <u>hot</u> outside.   (cold, warm)

3. I think we should <u>go</u> inside.   (work, stay)

4. I <u>stayed</u> in the car.   (left, thought)

Choosing the Right Meaning ▪ Write the letter of the correct meaning in each space.

top

a.   b.

_____ 1. He climbed to the top of the ladder.

_____ 2. Sara bought a top for her daughter.

_____ 3. That bowl is on the top shelf.

_____ 4. There is a closet at the top of the stairs.

_____ 5. Jamie is playing with a red top.

_____ 6. There is a green top in the toy box.

Vocabulary.   Read the directions with the students.

Sentences ▪ Underline the group of words that is a sentence.

1. Some people like to ride bikes.
   to ride bikes

2. Others like
   Others like to ice skate.

Word Order ▪ Rewrite each sentence correctly.

1. gets ready for work Sarah

_____

2. brushes She her teeth

_____

3. Sarah a shower takes

_____

4. She dries hair her

_____

5. puts on Sarah clothes her

_____

6. slips She on shoes her

_____

7. breakfast fixes She

_____

**Asking and Telling Sentences ▪ Read each sentence.
Write T if it is a telling sentence. Write A if it is an
asking sentence.**

_____ **1.** Rita is a vet.

_____ **2.** Does Rita like animals?

_____ **3.** Rita likes animals.

_____ **4.** Rita feeds the pets at her clinic.

_____ **5.** She takes good care of all the animals.

_____ **6.** Do you have a pet?

**Making Sentences ▪ Draw lines to match a naming
part with an action part. Then write the sentences on
the lines below.**

The sun		went for a walk.
The sky		blew slightly.
I		had fun.
My friend		was blue.
The wind		was shining.
We		went with me.

1. _____

2. _____

3. _____

4. _____

5. _____

6. _____

Naming Words and Action Words ▪ Underline the naming words. Circle the action words.

1. Gunnar walked to the store.

2. Miss Baker rode the bus to Elm City.

3. John plays the flute.

4. Lee drove home.

5. James works in the city.

Describing Words ▪ Circle the describing words.

1. The cute otter likes to play.

2. The otter is brown.

3. It swims in the cool water.

4. It has a green ball.

5. The ball is a new toy for the otter.

Using Is/Are and Was/Were ▪ Circle the word that best completes each sentence.

1. My friend (is, are) funny.

2. The women (is, are) laughing.

3. My dog (was, were) running.

4. The men (was, were) running, too.

5. Jeff (was, were) missing all of it.

6. We (was, were) having fun!

Using We, They, She, and He ▪ Rewrite the following sentences using We, They, She, and He.

1. Brad and I go bowling.

   _____

2. Shelly and Jared meet us there.

   _____

3. Shelly gets a strike.

   _____

4. Brad wins the game!

   _____

5. Shelly, Brad, and I need to leave.

   _____

6. Jared says good-bye to us.

   _____

7. Shelly, Brad, and I go home.

   _____

Using A or An ▪ Write a or an before each word.

1. _____ boat

2. _____ apple

3. _____ bus

4. _____ egg

5. _____ door

6. _____ uncle

7. _____ undershirt

8. _____ message

9. _____ inch

10. _____ oven

11. _____ aunt

12. _____ necklace

Writing Sentences Correctly ▪ Rewrite each sentence correctly. Use capital letters, periods, and question marks where needed.

1. ray worked with tony

_____

2. did they work on monday

_____

3. yes, they worked for juan

_____

4. i saw them in july

_____

5. do they live in chicago

_____

6. jim and i were born in may

_____

7. i met jim in new york

_____

8. liz will visit in april

_____

9. who is liz

_____

10. she is my cousin who lives in mexico

_____

11. she is taking an airplane

_____

Writing Sentences ▪ Write a sentence using each word. Use capital letters, periods, and question marks where needed.

1. september

_____

2. january

_____

3. may

_____

4. thursday

_____

5. saturday

_____

6. wednesday

_____

7. wisconsin

_____

8. boston

_____

9. japan

_____

10. austin

_____

11. august

_____

12. england

_____

Writing Sentences with Naming Words ▪ Use the naming words in the box to complete the sentences.

yarn	dog	food	cat	collar	trees	chair

1. Charlie is a black and white _____ .

2. He sleeps on the big brown _____ .

3. He plays with a ball of _____ .

4. His _____ is in his dish.

5. He likes to climb _____ .

6. He is afraid of our _____ .

7. He wears a red _____ .

Writing Sentences with Action Words ▪ Use the action words in the box to complete the sentences.

watch	makes	like	wash	reads	eat	tastes

1. Sharon _____ a pizza.

2. It _____ great!

3. They _____ every bite.

4. Tom _____ the newspaper.

5. Tom and Sharon _____ the dishes.

6. Then they _____ a movie together.

7. Tom and Sharon _____ the movie.

Composition.   Read the directions with the students.

Writing Sentences ▪ Write complete sentences to answer the questions.

1. Where were you born?

_____

2. What kind of job do you have?

_____

3. Do you like to read or write?

_____

4. Are you at school or at home?

_____

5. Do you like to wake up early or stay up late?

_____

6. Do you have a hobby?

_____

Writing a Letter ▪ Write the missing parts of the letter.

> Dear Andrew,   July 9, 1994
> Bob and Jan Mitchell   Yours truly,

1. _____

2. _____

   Thank you for inviting us to your house for dinner. We had a great time. We would like to have you over to our house for dinner next week. Please tell us which night is best for you.

3. _____

4. _____

A. Follow the directions given in each box.

1. Mark an X on the jar. 	**3.** Mark an X under the jar. 
2. Mark an X to the left of the jar. 	**4.** Draw a circle around the jar. 

B. Circle three things that are alike in some way.

C. Circle the photo that has a missing part. Draw the missing part.

Check What You've Learned. Read the directions with the students.

D. Circle the photo that is facing a different way.

E. Read the story. Then number the photos in the correct order.

Carl took some photos. First, he took a photo of an animal. Then he took one of a plant. Finally, he took a photo of a building.

_____   _____   _____

F. Write the missing letters.

1. L ___ ___ O P ___ R ___ T ___

2. c ___ e ___ g h ___ ___ k ___

G. Write the words in alphabetical order.

1. Barbara _____

   Robert _____

   Kamal _____

2. truck _____

   jeep _____

   car _____

Check What You've Learned.   Read the directions with the students.

113

H. Read the words in the box. Then follow the directions.

| three | come | see | call | give | below |

1. Write the word from the box that rhymes with each word.

tall _____   see _____

2. Write the word from the box that means almost the same as each word.

under _____   look _____

3. Write the word from the box that means the opposite of each word.

go _____   take _____

I. Write to or two to complete each sentence.

1. Jackie has _____ jobs.

2. She walks _____ both jobs.

J. Write T before the telling sentence. Write A before the asking sentence. Write X before the group of words that is not a sentence. Circle the naming words, and underline the action words in each sentence.

_____ 1. Terry has a

_____ 2. Terry goes in at noon.

_____ 3. Does the meeting start at one o'clock?

K. Circle the special naming words. Underline the action words. Write T before the sentence if the action word happens today. Write Y before the sentence that has an action word for yesterday.

_____ 1. I called Sarah.

_____ 2. She drove to Houston.

_____ 3. Dean rides with her to Houston.

_____ 4. They go every Friday.

Check What You've Learned.   Read the directions with the students.

114

L. Circle the word that best completes each sentence.

1. Tom (is, are) going to the bus stop.

2. (She, He) sees the bus stop is empty.

3. Tom (was, were) late and missed the bus.

4. Tom took (a, an) taxi.

M. Circle each letter that should be a capital letter. Add the correct punctuation mark at the end of each sentence.

1. sharita took her cat, fluffy, to the vet in cedar creek

2. when did she take her cat to dr. quincy

3. sharita and i drove there last friday

N. Write complete sentences to answer the questions.

1. Do you like going to movies or going shopping?

_____

2. Do you like to cook or to garden?

_____

Below is a list of sections on *Check What You've Learned* and the pages on which the skills in each section are taught. If you missed any questions, turn to the pages listed, and practice the skills. Then correct the problems you missed on *Check What You've Learned*.

Section	Practice Page	Section	Practice Page	Section	Practice Page
Unit 1		F	17–19	*Unit 4*	
A	5–6	G	20	K	51–59
B	7	*Unit 2*		L	60–61, 63, 66–67
C	11	H	26–31	*Unit 5*	
D	12	I	33	M	74–83
E	13–15	*Unit 3*		*Unit 6*	
		J	38–46	N	89–92

Check What You've Learned. Read the directions with the students. Help students use the *Check What You've Learned Correlation Chart* to assess the skills they need to work on.

Check What You Know (P. 1)

A. The answers should be marked as follows:
1. mark an X̱ on the desk
2. mark an X̱ to the right of the desk
3. mark an X̱ over the desk
4. draw a circle around the desk

B. The car should not be circled.

C. The watch with part of the band missing should be circled. The missing part of the band should be drawn.

Check What You Know (P. 2)

D. The fourth fork should be circled.

E. The photos should be numbered as follows:
1, milk
2, vegetables
3, bread

F. 1. B, C, D, E, F, G, H, I, J, K
2. Q, R, S, T, U, V, W, X, Y, Z
3. r, s, t, u, v, w, x, y, z
4. c, d, e, f, g, h, i, j, k, l

G. 1. Adam
Darrell
Jake
2. eye
nose
toe

Check What You Know (P. 3)

H. 1. shoe, fan
2. little, happy
3. up, thin

I. 1. to
2. two

J. The words in bold should be circled.
1. A, Can you go to the **store** for me?
2. T, I need **eggs** and **bread**.
3. X

K. The words in bold should be circled.
1. T, **Mr. Kelso** helps at **Bayview Hospital**.
2. T, He lives close to the hospital.
3. Y, Last year **Mrs. Kelso** worked at the hospital.
4. Y, She retired this year.

Check What You Know (P. 4)

L. 1. were
2. We
3. an
4. are

M. The letters in bold should be circled.
1. **k**endall and **i** shopped at **s**unshine **m**all last **t**hursday.
2. **r**osa has not been there since **d**ecember.
3. **i**s that where **r**osa got her dog, **b**rownie?

N. Discuss your answers with your instructor.
1. I like (walking, driving).
2. I like to shop at the (book store, music store).

Lesson 1, Following Directions (P. 5)

The following should be marked:
1. X on the pot
2. X above the pot
3. X below the pot
4. X to the right of the pot
5. X to the left of the pot
6. X inside the pot
7. X on the handle of the pot
8. a circle around the pot

Lesson 2, More About Following Directions (P. 6)

These photos should be circled:
1. the book on the left
2. the watch on the right
3. the rose on the left
4. the clock on the left
5. the toaster on the right

Lesson 3, Finding the One That Is the Same (P. 7)

These photos should be circled:
1. third photo in the row: ax
2. second photo in the row: pot
3. second photo in the row: sewing needle without thread
4. third photo in the row: bed with a headboard
5. third photo in the row: tea kettle with a handle
6. fourth photo in the row: four tools

Lesson 4, Finding the One That Is Different (P. 8)

These photos should be circled:
1. fourth box—can without a lid
2. second box—TV without an antenna
3. third box—pan without a handle
4. fourth box—kite without a tail
5. second box—kitten
6. first box—umbrella without a handle

Lesson 5, Complete the Groups (P. 9)

These photos should be circled:
1. grapefruit
2. cat
3. jeep
4. fork
5. jacket

Lesson 6, Putting Things in Groups (P. 10)

These photos should be circled:
1. goat, dog, otter
2. motorcycle helmet, hat, cap
3. bed, desk, table
4. darts, football, fishing rod
5. dress, socks, jeans

Lesson 7, Adding Missing Parts (P. 11)

These photos should be circled, and the missing parts should be drawn:
1. third firecracker—missing the fuse
2. first gas pump—missing the hose
3. second group of dishes—missing the bowls in back
4. second safety pin—missing one side
5. third combination lock—missing the loop

Lesson 8, Reversals (P. 12)

These photos should be circled:
1. fourth bat
2. second fan
3. third key
4. first pitcher
5. second car

Lesson 9, Listening for Information (P. 13)

The following should be marked with an X:
1. second picture
2. first picture
3. second picture
4. third picture

Lesson 10, Remembering the Order (P. 14)

Photos should be numbered as follows:
1. 1, man working on his car
   2, man walking with books in his hand
   3, man at the library
   4, man making pizza
2. 1, woman on the phone
   2, woman talking to the man without the ladder
   3, woman letting in the man with the ladder
   4, woman letting in another woman

Lesson 11, Listening and Thinking (P. 15)

These photos should be marked with an X:
1. pitcher
2. tree
3. vase
4. bread
5. mop
6. knife
7. pencil
8. ham

Lesson 12, Comparing Letters (P. 16)

These letters should be circled:

Top:
1. B
2. I
3. O
4. E
5. C
6. N
7. P
8. U
9. T
10. Q
11. W
12. D

Bottom:
1. b
2. t
3. v
4. r
5. g
6. m
7. f
8. q
9. n
10. e
11. y
12. h

Lesson 13, Missing Capital Letters (P. 17)

Discuss your answers with your instructor.

Lesson 14, Missing Small Letters (P. 18)

Discuss your answers with your instructor.

Lesson 15, Putting Letters in Alphabetical Order (P. 19)

Top:
1. A, B
2. X, Y
3. G, H
4. C, D
5. Q, R
6. J, K
7. L, M
8. Y, Z
9. Q, R
10. P, Q
11. B, C, D, E
12. M, N, O, P
13. S, T, U, V
14. G, H, I, J
15. J, K, L, M
16. P, Q, R, S
17. V, W, X, Y
18. T, U, V, W

Bottom:
1. b, c
2. g, h
3. t, u
4. p, q
5. j, k
6. b, c
7. t, u
8. e, f
9. n, o
10. y, z
11. c, d, e, f
12. p, q, r, s
13. m, n, o, p
14. f, g, h, i
15. h, i, j, k
16. e, f, g, h
17. t, u, v, w
18. o, p, q, r

Lesson 16, Putting Words in Alphabetical Order (P. 20)

1. bird, cat, dog, frog
2. just, know, like, me
3. she, they, we, you
4. find, give, help, is
5. left, near, on, quick
6. most, name, one, red

Review (P. 21)

Answers should be marked as follows:
1. circle the bed, table, and desk
2. circle the belt
3. mark an X on the second flower
4. circle the second elephant; draw that elephant's trunk
5. mark an X on the fourth nurse
6. mark an X on the second hose

Review (P. 22)

Top:
1. 1, doctor with man
   2, doctor with woman who has crutches
   3, doctor talking to woman

The following should be marked:
2. circle the M's
3. circle B
4. mark an X on p
5. circle i

Middle:
1. C, D, E
2. G, H, I
3. Q, R, S
4. a, b, c
5. m, n, o
6. v, w, x

Bottom:
1. at   2. go
   in   stop
   on   turn

Using What You've Learned (P. 23)

Answers should be marked as follows:

Top:

1. mark an X on top of the computer
2. mark an X on the chair that is different
3. circle the notebooks that are the same

Bottom:

1. mark an X on the smaller envelope
2. mark an X on the eraser on the right
3. draw a box around the two small ($3\frac{1}{2}$ inch) diskettes

Using What You've Learned (P. 24)

Answers should be marked as follows:

Section 1:

1. mark an X on the jacket
2. mark an X on the car

Section 2:

1. A, B
2. M, N
3. Q, R
4. E, F
5. N, O
6. R, S
7. F, G, H
8. V, W, X
9. D, E, F

Section 3:

1. g, h
2. p, q
3. y, z
4. b, c
5. l, m
6. h, i
7. m, n, o
8. s, t, u
9. a, b, c

Section 4:

1. Anna
   Pat
   Tom
2. Ellen
   Lynn
   Raul

 Unit 2 Vocabulary

Lesson 17, Naming Sounds (P. 25)

These photos should be circled:

1. keys
2. tea kettle
3. telephone
4. radio
5. quarterback
6. woman sneezing
7. elevator
8. woman yelling

Lesson 18, Rhyming Words (P. 26)

1. bat — hat
2. bone — cone
3. fan — man
4. nail — mail
5. dog — log
6. mice — rice

Lesson 19, More Rhyming Words (P. 27)

1. mop
2. fan
3. mat
4. rug
5. log
6. sun
7. gate

Lesson 20, Words with Like Meanings (P. 28)

The following should be circled:

Top:

1. little, small
2. start, begin
3. stop, finish
4. sound, noise

5. high, tall
6. narrow, thin
7. look, see
8. large, big
9. below, under
10. all, every
11. happy, glad
12. easy, simple

Bottom:
1. small
2. big
3. repairing
4. below
5. write
6. finish
7. begin
8. noise

Lesson 21, Words with Like Meanings (P. 29)

1. sound, noise
2. begin, starts
3. see, watch
4. glad, happy
5. ended, finished
6. little, small
7. likes, enjoys
8. heard, listened
9. under, below
10. big, large

Lesson 22, Words with Opposite Meanings (P. 30)

Top:
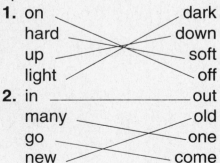
1. on — dark
   hard — down
   up — soft
   light — off
2. in — out
   many — old
   go — one
   new — come

3. sink — thick
   tall — back
   thin — float
   front — short
4. good — dry
   wide — bad
   find — lose
   wet — narrow

Bottom:
1. back
2. new
3. dirty
4. sad
5. down
6. hard
7. light
8. off

Lesson 23, Words with Opposite Meanings (P. 31)

1. short, tall
2. dark, light
3. opened, closed
4. out, in
5. old, new
6. in, out
7. up, down
8. hard, soft
9. now, later
10. day, night

Lesson 24, Choosing the Right Meaning (P. 32)

1. a
2. b
3. a
4. b
5. a
6. b
7. b
8. a
9. a

10. b
11. b
12. a
13. b
14. b

Lesson 25, Writing Words That Sound Alike (P. 33)

Top:
1. I took a chair to Ben.
2. Ben came over to eat dinner.
3. He will wait to eat dessert.
4. He wants to help wash the dishes.

Middle:
1. There are two women.
2. They have worked together for two years.
3. They each have two meetings.
4. They need to have two things ready for the meetings.

Bottom:
1. two
2. to
3. two
4. to

Review (P. 34)

Answers should be marked as follows:

Section 1:
1. X on the zipper
2. X on the phone

Section 2:
1. star, car
2. log, fog
3. tug, rug

4. boat, float
5. mouse, house
6. sat, hat
7. run, sun
8. when, ten

Section 3:
1. hard — soft
   up — down
   old — new
   push — pull

2. in — out
   go — come
   light — dark
   on — off

Section 4:
1. little — big
   stop — end
   large — small
   start — begin

2. sound — noise
   look — see
   print — write
   below — under

Review (P. 35)

Top:
1. b
2. a
3. b
4. a
5. b
6. a
7. a
8. b

Bottom:
1. two
2. to
3. to

4. two
5. to
6. two
7. to
8. to

Using What You've Learned (P. 36)

Top:
1. man
2. came
3. town
4. tall
5. dark
6. nice
7. read

Bottom:
1. two
2. to
3. two
4. to
5. two
6. two
7. to

Using What You've Learned (P. 37)

Top:
1. book, look
2. say, day
3. dog, log
4. dig, big
5. fan, man
6. rug, bug
7. see, me
8. cat, mat

Middle:
1. look, see
2. little, small
3. tall, high
4. happy, glad
5. skinny, thin

6. tell, say
7. near, close
8. big, large

Bottom:
1. on, off
2. come, go
3. in, out
4. old, new
5. up, down
6. go, stop
7. hard, soft
8. smooth, bumpy

Unit 3 Sentences

Lesson 26, Sentences (P. 38)

The following sentences should be underlined:
1. The Perez family needs a house.
2. They choose this one.
3. Anthony wants a new job.
4. Mr. Barker asks the questions.
5. Joanne calls a friend.
6. She talks to Frank.

Lesson 27, Word Order in Sentences (P. 39)

The following sentences should be underlined and written:
1. Max walks home.
2. He plays the radio.
3. He is late.
4. He opens the door.
5. Max is hungry.
6. He makes dinner.
7. Max sets the table.
8. The phone rings.
9. Max picks it up.
10. No one is there.
11. Max sits down.

Lesson 28, More Word Order in Sentences (P. 40)

1. Richard jogs quickly.
2. I cannot swim.
3. Pablo likes driving.
4. He drives a truck.
5. Mike likes his job.
6. He is good at it.
7. Eva walks to town.
8. Ms. Fisher got a book.
9. It is due today.
10. Mr. Kim sees a bird.
11. It is red.
12. There is its nest.

Lesson 29, Sentences That Tell (P. 41)

1. I went to the mountains.
2. I went with a friend.
3. We went camping.
4. We stayed in a tent.
5. The weather was great.
6. We stayed for one week.
7. I built a campfire.
8. We cooked our food over the fire.
9. My friend took pictures.

Lesson 30, Sentences That Ask (P. 42)

1. What is your name?
2. What are you studying?
3. Where do you live?
4. How do I get there?
5. What is your phone number?
6. Where do you work?
7. What kind of work do you do?
8. Do you like your job?
9. What time do you finish work?

Lesson 31, Telling or Asking Sentences (P. 43)

2, 4, 5, 7, and 10 should be circled.

1, 3, 6, 8, 9, and 11 should be marked with an X.

1. I got a new car.
2. Do you like it?
3. We can go for a drive.
4. Where would you like to go?
5. Will you drive me to the store?
6. I can drive you to the store.
7. Have you seen my keys?
8. I can't find them.
9. You left them in the car.
10. Are you sure?
11. Yes, I can see them.

Lesson 32, Sentence Parts That Name (P. 44)

1. Rick
2. the monkey
3. the bear
4. the lions
5. the tiger
6. Rick's son
7. the pink birds
8. the turtle
9. the owl
10. Rick's daughter

Lesson 33, Sentence Parts That Show Action (P. 45)

1. found a dog
2. ate some food
3. licked Mrs. Hanson's hand
4. named the dog Skip
5. threw a ball
6. ran after the ball
7. got the ball
8. took a nap
9. took Skip to the vet
10. gave Skip a shot

Lesson 34, Combining Sentence Parts (P. 46)

Sentences may vary. Suggested sentences:

Top:
1. Dan fed the dog.
2. The dog ate the food.
3. I helped Dan.
4. Dan and his dog took a walk.
5. Dan's dog wanted to run.

Bottom:
1. Pat has two new mice.
2. She thinks they are very cute.
3. The mice are very small.
4. They are easy to keep as pets.
5. Many people don't like mice.

Review (P. 47)
Top:

The following should be underlined:
1. Mr. Dawson walks Anna home.
2. She takes out her keys.
3. Anna unlocks the door.
4. She waves to Mr. Dawson.
5. Mr. Dawson waves back.

Bottom:
The following sentences should be written:
1. Mr. Dawson is Anna's boss.
2. Anna likes her boss.
3. He is nice.
4. Mr. Dawson leaves.
5. Anna goes into her house.
6. She will see him tomorrow.
7. She starts dinner.
8. She will eat soon.

Review (P. 48)
Top:
1. A
2. T
3. A
4. T
5. A
6. T
7. T
8. A
9. T
10. A
11. T
12. A

Bottom:
1. The room is very crowded.
2. The woman is holding a cup.
3. The people are talking to each other.

Using What You've Learned (P. 49)

Discuss your answers with your instructor.

Using What You've Learned (P. 50)

Sentences may vary. A possible story follows.
1. The school is close to my house.
2. I go to school two times each week.
3. The classroom has many windows.
4. The library is full of books.
5. Our class works hard.
6. My teacher helps me learn new things.
7. My friend is in the same class.
8. We take our books to class.
9. Many students go back to school.
10. They hope to get better jobs.

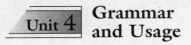

Lesson 35, Naming Words (P. 51)

1. family, man, woman
2. store, city, house
3. car, fish, apple
4. clock, book, watch

Lesson 36, Two Kinds of Naming Words (P. 52)

Top:

These special naming words should be circled:

1. Pat
2. Mary
3. Sara
4. Tony
5. Ann
6. Lee Chin
7. Scott
8. Ms. Alba
9. Mr. Ross
10. Dr. Brown

Bottom:

People	Special Names
1. man	1. Pat
2. woman	2. Mary
3. baby	3. Sara
4. son	4. Tony
5. daughter	5. Ann
6. sister	6. Lee Chin
7. brother	7. Scott
8. friend	8. Ms. Alba
9. neighbor	9. Mr. Ross
10. doctor	10. Dr. Brown

Lesson 37, More Naming Words (P. 53)

Top:

These special naming words should be circled:

1. Kansas City
2. First Street
3. The Rental Place
4. Peace Park
5. Sun Beach
6. Elm Library
7. City Books
8. Bank of Missouri
9. Memorial Hospital
10. Parkview Apartments

Bottom:

Places

1. city
2. street
3. office
4. park
5. beach
6. library
7. store
8. bank
9. hospital
10. apartment

Special Places

1. Kansas City
2. First Street
3. The Rental Place
4. Peace Park
5. Sun Beach
6. Elm Library
7. City Books
8. Bank of Missouri
9. Memorial Hospital
10. Parkview Apartments

Lesson 38, One and More Than One (P. 54)

Top:
1. radios
2. pencils
3. books
4. nests
5. dogs
6. forks

Bottom:
1. legs
2. head
3. ears
4. eyes
5. nose

Lesson 39, Action Words (P. 55)
1. meet **or** talk
2. grow
3. eat **or** talk
4. talk
5. cheer
6. shop **or** talk
7. jog **or** talk
8. paint **or** talk

Lesson 40, Using Action Words (P. 56)

Top:
1. need
2. go
3. talk
4. asks
5. sells
6. writes

Bottom:
1. likes
2. takes
3. learn
4. help
5. holds
6. looks

Lesson 41, Action Words with One or More (P. 57)

Top:
The letters in bold should be circled.
1. The woman work**s**.
   The women work.
2. The dog jump**s**.
   The dogs jump.
3. The doorbell ring**s**.
   The doorbells ring.
4. The clock work**s** well.
   The clocks work well.
5. The man walk**s** slowly.
   The men walk slowly.
6. The car honk**s**.
   The cars honk.
7. The horse run**s** fast.
   The horses run fast.
8. The plant grow**s** quickly.
   The plants grow quickly.

Bottom:
1. work; works
2. blows; blow
3. rolls; roll
4. write; writes
5. thinks, think

Lesson 42, Action Words for Today (P. 58)
1. plays; learns
2. walks; climbs
3. jumps; walks
4. jogs; talks
5. fixes; enjoys
6. trains; hopes
7. works; likes

Lesson 43, Action Words for Yesterday (P. 59)

1. played; learned
2. walked; climbed
3. jumped; walked
4. jogged; talked
5. fixed; enjoyed
6. trained; hoped
7. worked; liked

Lesson 44, Using *Is* or *Are* (P. 60)

1. is
2. is
3. are
4. are
5. is
6. is
7. is
8. are
9. are
10. is
11. is
12. are
13. is
14. are
15. are
16. is
17. are
18. are

Lesson 45, Using *Was* or *Were* (P. 61)

1. was
2. was
3. were
4. were
5. was
6. was
7. was
8. was
9. was
10. were
11. were
12. were
13. was
14. was
15. was
16. was
17. was
18. were

Lesson 46, Using *See, Come,* and *Run* (P. 62)

Top:
1. see
2. saw
3. see
4. ran
5. saw
6. run
7. run
8. ran
9. run
10. come
11. came
12. come

Bottom:
1. I see a pretty picture now.
2. Last night Kim ran fast.
3. Then she came to see me.

Lesson 47, Using *She* and *He* (P. 63)

1. She has a pencil.
2. He has a book.
3. She writes with the pencil.
4. He reads the book.
5. She enjoys writing stories.
6. He likes to read stories.
7. He finishes the book.

Lesson 48, Using *We* and *They* (P. 64)

1. We are here.
2. They are not here yet.
3. They are late.
4. They might miss the race.
5. We are on time.
6. We will be in the race.
7. They get there just in time.

Lesson 49, Using *I* (P. 65)

1. Jim and I go to the pond.
2. The park is not far from where I live.
3. Jim and I go there to fish.
4. Jim and I always have a good time there.
5. I sit on the grass.
6. I sit by Jim.
7. I take out my fishing rod.
8. I help Jim put a worm on his hook.
9. Jim and I catch fish.
10. I look at the water.
11. I can see some other fish.
12. Jim and I have fun.
13. I caught four fish.
14. Jim and I caught ten fish in all.
15. I put the fish in a bucket.

Lesson 50, Using *An* (P. 66)

Section 1:

1. a, e, i, o, u

Section 2:

1. an
2. an
3. an
4. an

Section 3:

1. an
2. an
4. an
6. an
7. an

Section 4:

2. an
4. an
6. an

Lesson 51, Using *A* or *An* (P. 67)

Top:
The letters b, c, d, f, g, h, j, k, l, m, n, p, q, r, s, t, v, w, x, y, and z should be circled.

1. a
2. a
3. a
4. a
5. an
6. an
7. a
8. a

Bottom:
Discuss your answers with your instructor.

Lesson 52, Using Describing Words (P. 68)

The following words should be circled and written:

Top:

1. noisy
2. happy
3. shiny
4. hungry
5. cold
6. mad

Bottom:

1. noisy
2. happy
3. shiny
4. hungry
5. cold
6. mad

Lesson 53, Using More Describing Words (P. 69)

These words should be circled:
1. big, old, black, brown, white, soft
2. large, heavy, white, empty
3. new, red
4. red, shiny, sweet, good

Review (P. 70)

Section 1:
The following words should be underlined:
1. Miss Taylor, children, circus
2. elephants, tent

Section 2:
The following words should be circled:
1. watched
2. laughed

Section 3:
The following words should be boxed:
1. funny, big
2. happy, small

Section 4:
The following words should be circled:
1. Pepi
2. Leo
3. Blaze
4. Flipper

Section 5:

Animals	Special Names
1. dog	1. Pepi
2. cat	2. Leo
3. horse	3. Blaze
4. fish	4. Flipper

Review (P. 71)

Top:
1. cars
2. bananas
3. desks
4. books

Middle:
1. are
2. is
3. see
4. saw
5. are
6. was
7. Are
8. run

Bottom:
1. John — she
2. Sue — he
3. Sue and John — we
4. Bill and I — they

Using What You've Learned (P. 72)

Top:
1. are
2. walks
3. walks
4. worked
5. pulled
6. planted
7. watered
8. were

Bottom:
1. They are in the park.
2. He walks very quickly.
3. She walks slower than Tim.
4. They worked in the yard yesterday.
5. He pulled the weeds.
6. She planted some seeds.
7. He watered the seeds.
8. They were tired after working all day.

Using What You've Learned (P. 73)

1. is; a
2. an; a
3. is; He
4. work; They
5. live; walk
6. rides; She

Lesson 54, Beginning a Sentence (P. 74)

Top:

The first letter should be underlined in the following words:

1. Mark
2. There
3. Which
4. It
5. Mark
6. He
7. It
8. How

Bottom:

1. The sun is hot.
2. We will go home.
3. Can you come with us?
4. We will get some water.
5. What time is it?

Lesson 55, Writing Names of People (P. 75)

Top:
1. Josie
2. Mr. Collins

Bottom:
1. Pat Long
2. Eva Ramos
3. Bill Adams
4. Will Brown
5. Mr. Franklin
6. Mrs. Douglas
7. Ms. Baxter
8. Dr. Butala

Lesson 56, Writing Names of Pets (P. 76)

Answers may vary. All names should be capitalized. Suggested answers:

1. Tiger
2. Chip
3. Speedy
4. Goldy
5. King
6. Jet

Lesson 57, Writing Names of Days (P. 77)

1. Monday
2. Friday
3. Sunday
4. Tuesday
5. Tuesday, Thursday
6. Saturday, Sunday
7. Wednesday
8. Friday, Saturday

Lesson 58, Writing Names of Months (P. 78)

1. January
2. February
3. March
4. April
5. May
6. June
7. July
8. August
9. September
10. October
11. November
12. December

Lesson 59, Writing Names of Places (P. 79)

Top:
1. Bob lives on Jones Street.
2. He works on River Road.
3. I live on Oak Street.
4. I work on Lake Drive.
5. My bank is on First Street.

Bottom:
1. Diane lives in Dallas.
2. She came from Paris.
3. My home is in Montreal.
4. My friend lives in Boston.
5. Have you ever been to Kansas City?

Lesson 60, Writing I (P. 80)

Discuss your answers with your instructor.

Lesson 61, Ending a Telling Sentence (P. 81)

Top:
1. Lisa looks at the photos.
2. She keeps them in a book.
3. The photos are of Lisa's family.
4. Some of the photos are old.
5. Other photos are new.
6. Lisa puts new photos in the book every year.
7. The photos are special to Lisa.

Bottom:
1. This is my home.
2. I cut the grass.
3. Next, I rake it.
4. Then I pull the weeds.
5. It looks good.
6. I put my tools away.

Lesson 62, Ending an Asking Sentence (P. 82)

Top:
1. Will I get that new job?
2. When will I find out about it?
3. Who will call me?
4. Should I call to ask about the job?
5. What will my new job be like?
6. What will my new office look like?
7. How much money will I make?

Bottom:
1. Who said my name?
2. Was it Bud?
3. Did Bud go home?
4. When will he come back?
5. Isn't his car broken down?
6. How did he get home?

Lesson 63, Ending Sentences (P. 83)

1. .; Our town often floods.
2. .; The river gets too full.
3. ?; Will the river flood today?
4. .; It floods whenever it rains.
5. ?; How can we stop the floods?
6. ?; Should we build a dam?
7. .; A dam will help stop the floods.
8. ?; How long will it take to build the dam?
9. .; It will take one year to build.

Lesson 64, Writing Dates (P. 84)

1. February 14, 1994
2. January 1, 1993
3. October 31, 1991
4. November 23, 1993
5. July 4, 1993
6. August 9, 1994
7. April 12, 1994
8. May 5, 1994
9. Discuss your answer with your instructor.

Review (P. 85)

1. .; Joe Garza and I ride to work together.
2. .; We will be off on Friday.
3. ?; Did Joe call his brother, Ray?
4. .; Last Friday I called Ray.
5. ?; Do you work on Monday?
6. .; I work on Monday.
7. .; Ray will visit in September.
8. .; He is coming from Toronto.
9. ?; How long will he stay?

Review (P. 86)

1. I saw Sue.
2. She lives on Lee Road.
3. She was born May 1, 1958.
4. Her dog is named Wags.
5. Wags is a friendly dog.
6. Sue is a doctor.
7. Her office is on First Street.
8. She is a good doctor.
9. Many people visit her.
10. Sue is always busy.

Using What You've Learned (P. 87)

Discuss your answers with your instructor.

Using What You've Learned (P. 88)

1. Where is Bill?
2. He is in the house.
3. He just got home.
4. Bill has two cookies.
5. What is Bill doing?
6. He is making a snack.
7. Can he cook?
8. What is he making?
9. The snack is sweet.
10. It is a good snack.
11. Would you like some?
12. Yes, I would.
13. This is really good.

Unit 6   Composition

Lesson 65, Sentences with Naming Words (P. 89)

Sentences may vary. Suggested answers:

1. store
2. seeds
3. garden
4. day
5. weeds
6. rain
7. sun
8. flowers
9. vegetables
10. basket
11. soup
12. neighbor
13. friend
14. table
15. plants

Lesson 66, Sentences with Action Words (P. 90)

Sentences may vary. Suggested answers:

1. live
2. shop
3. read
4. find
5. cut
6. opens
7. needs
8. lifts
9. write
10. take
11. ask
12. likes
13. buy
14. want
15. chooses

Lesson 67, Writing Sentences (P. 91)

Discuss your answers with your instructor.

1. I am a (man, woman).
2. I am (working, relaxing).
3. I use a (pen, pencil).
4. I (walk, drive) to work.
5. I like (grapes, raisins).
6. I live in (a house, an apartment).
7. I (cook, go out to eat).
8. I (watch TV, read books).

Lesson 68, Writing More Sentences (P. 92)

Sentences may vary. Suggested answers:

Top:

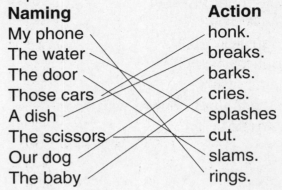

Naming	Action
My phone	honk.
The water	breaks.
The door	barks.
Those cars	cries.
A dish	splashes
The scissors	cut.
Our dog	slams.
The baby	rings.

Bottom:

1. My phone rings.
2. The water splashes.
3. The door slams.
4. Those cars honk.
5. A dish breaks.
6. The scissors cut.
7. Our dog barks.
8. The baby cries.

Lesson 69, A Thank-You Letter (P. 93)

Top:

1. Dear Janet,
2. Dear Mother,
3. Dear Tom,
4. Dear Ms. Roberts,
5. Dear Mr. Chang,

Bottom:

1. Your friend,
   (Discuss your answer with your instructor.)
2. Love,
   Aaron
3. Sincerely,
   Michelle
4. Yours truly,
   Dawn

Lesson 70, Writing a Thank-You Letter (P. 94)

        May 1, 19___ (dates will vary)

Dear Mr. Green,

   Thank you for the book you sent to me about recycling. It was very helpful and interesting. Please send me one of your new catalogs.

        Yours truly,
        Anthony Perez

Lesson 71, Writing a Poem (P. 95)

The following words should be circled:

Top:
near; year
bold; old
day; say

Middle:
trip
done

Bottom:
play
hear

Review (P. 96)

Top:
1. letters
2. write
3. trip
4. drove
5. visited
6. play

Bottom:
Discuss your answers with your instructor.

1. I like (chocolate, vanilla) ice cream.
2. It is (sunny, rainy) today.
3. I like to read (stories, poems).
4. I live (close to, far away from) my job.
5. I like (football, baseball).
6. I am (tall, short).

Review (P. 97)

Top:
1. C
2. D
3. A
4. B

Bottom
1. cab   sock
2. bank   well
3. clock   mug
4. stuck   cheap
5. week   fill
6. sell   dice
7. sleep   truck
8. price   grab
9. spill   speak
10. rug   drank

Using What You've Learned (P. 98)

Top:
Answers will vary. Suggested answers:
1. The men meet at five o'clock.
2. The friends walk out the door.
3. Three people jog in the park.
4. The amusement park closes at six o'clock.
5. The dog barks at the cat in a tree.
6. Two women talk about work.
7. Four friends stop at the fountain.
8. My boss leaves the same time I do.

Bottom:
Discuss your answers with your instructor.

Using What You've Learned (P. 99)

May 5, 19____ (dates will vary)

Dear Mr. Jefferson,

Thank you for talking to me about the clinic I would like to open. You have given me some good ideas. Our town needs a clinic to help sick people. I would like to start building it as soon as possible.

Sincerely,
Dr. Sharon Turner

 Final Reviews

Final Review, Unit 1 (P. 100)

The following should be marked:

Section 1:

1. circle the basketball, baseball, and football; mark an X on the book
2. circle the saw, hammer, and wrench; mark an X on the hammer

Section 2:

1. mark an X on the third photo

Section 3:

1. circle the weather vane without the arrow; draw the arrow
2. circle the cup without a handle; draw the handle

Section 4:

1. mark an X on the second photo
2. mark an X on the third photo

Final Review, Unit 1 (P. 101)

Top:

The photos should be numbered as follows:

1. 1, woman at the store
   2, man helping woman bring packages into the kitchen
   3, man and woman cooking at the stove

Middle:

1. B
2. L
3. P
4. h
5. n
6. w

Bottom:

1. Diane
   Ling
   Maria
2. car
   rain
   woman
3. fly
   house
   man
4. lake
   truck
   zoo

Final Review, Unit 2 (P. 102)

Top:

The following photos should be marked with an X:

1. alarm clock
2. fan
3. TV
4. gas pump

Bottom:

The following should be circled:

1. Pat, sat, mat
2. bug, rug
3. hop, mop
4. bear, pear
5. bee, tree
6. fun, sun
7. light, night
8. coat, boat
9. wait, gate
10. mouse, house

Final Review, Unit 2 (P. 103)

Top:

The following words should be circled:

1. large, big
2. go, leave
3. print, write
4. high, tall
5. start, begin
6. small, little

Middle:

1. open
2. cold
3. stay
4. left

Bottom:

1. b
2. a
3. b
4. b
5. a
6. a

Final Review, Unit 3 (P. 104)

Top:

The following sentences should be underlined:

1. Some people like to ride bikes.
2. Others like to ice skate.

Bottom:

1. Sarah gets ready for work.
2. She brushes her teeth.
3. Sarah takes a shower.
4. She dries her hair.
5. Sarah puts on her clothes. **or** Sarah puts her clothes on.
6. She slips on her shoes.
7. She fixes breakfast.

Final Review, Unit 3 (P. 105)

Top:

1. T
2. A
3. T
4. T
5. T
6. A

Bottom:

Answers may vary. Suggested answers:

1. The sun was shining.
2. The sky was blue.
3. I went for a walk.
4. My friend went with me.
5. The wind blew slightly.
6. We had fun.

Final Review, Unit 4 (P. 106)

Top:

The words in bold should be circled.

1. Gunnar **walked** to the store.
2. Miss Baker **rode** the bus to Elm City.
3. John **plays** the flute.
4. Lee **drove** home.
5. James **works** in the city.

Middle:

The words in bold should be circled.

1. The **cute** otter likes to play.
2. The otter is **brown**.
3. It swims in the **cool** water.
4. It has a **green** ball.
5. The ball is a **new** toy for the otter.

Bottom:

1. is
2. are
3. was
4. were
5. was
6. were

Final Review, Unit 4 (P. 107)

Top:
1. We go bowling.
2. They meet us there.
3. She gets a strike.
4. He wins the game!
5. We need to leave.
6. He says good-bye to us.
7. We go home.

Bottom:
1. a
2. an
3. a
4. an
5. a
6. an
7. an
8. a
9. an
10. an
11. an
12. a

Final Review, Unit 5 (P. 108)

1. Ray worked with Tony.
2. Did they work on Monday?
3. Yes, they worked for Juan.
4. I saw them in July.
5. Do they live in Chicago?
6. Jim and I were born in May.
7. I met Jim in New York.
8. Liz will visit in April.
9. Who is Liz?
10. She is my cousin who lives in Mexico.
11. She is taking an airplane.

Final Review, Unit 5 (P. 109)

Discuss your answers with your instructor.

Final Review, Unit 6 (P. 110)

Top:
1. cat
2. chair
3. yarn
4. food
5. trees
6. dog
7. collar

Bottom:
1. makes
2. tastes
3. eat
4. reads
5. wash
6. watch
7. like

Final Review, Unit 6 (P. 111)

Top:

Discuss your answers with your instructor.
1. I was born in _____.
2. I work as a _____.
3. I like to (read, write).
4. I am at (school, home).
5. I like to (wake up early, stay up late).
6. I (have, do not have) a hobby.

Bottom:
1. July 9, 1994
2. Dear Andrew,
3. Yours truly,
4. Bob and Jan Mitchell

Check What You've Learned (P. 112)

A. The answers should be marked as follows:
1. mark an X on the jar
2. mark an X̄ to the left of the jar
3. mark an X̱ under the jar
4. draw a circle around the jar

B. The wall clock, alarm clock, and watch should be circled.

C. The pan without a handle should be circled. The handle on the pan should be drawn.

Check What You've Learned (P. 113)

D. The first stove should be circled.

E. The photos should be numbered as follows:
1, dog
2, rose
3, house

F. 1. L, M, N, O, P, Q, R, S, T, U
2. c, d, e, f, g, h, i, j, k, l

G. 1. Barbara
Kamal
Robert
2. car
jeep
truck

Check What You've Learned (P. 114)

H. 1. call, three
2. below, see
3. come, give

I. 1. two
2. to

J. The words in bold should be circled.
1. X
2. T, **Terry** goes in at **noon**.
3. A, Does the **meeting** start at one **o'clock**?

K. The words in bold should be circled.
1. Y, I called **Sarah**.
2. Y, She drove to **Houston**.
3. T, **Dean** rides with her to **Houston**.
4. T, They go every **Friday**.

Check What You've Learned (P. 115)

L. 1. is
2. He
3. was
4. a

M. The letters in bold should be circled.
1. **s**harita took her cat, **f**luffy, to the vet in **c**edar **c**reek.
2. **w**hen did she take her cat to **d**r. **q**uincy?
3. **s**harita and **i** drove there last **f**riday.

N. Discuss your answers with your instructor.
1. I like (going to movies, going shopping).
2. I like (to cook, to garden).